TABLE OF CONTE

Notes for a Magazine 3
ANNEMARIE MONAHAN
Agnes 5
GIZELLE S.
a feminist kind of sex 21
in exile 23
the first sin 24
ROBERTA ARNOLD, PHYLLIS BLOOM, REENI GOLDIN, M. PATRICIA
YASIN ORENDA THIE ÍE KA:KEN
1971 Dyke Outlaw Road Trip 25
BONNILEE KAUFMAN
Richter Scale 51
CATHY MARSTON, PHD
For Molly/Eulogy for a Prisoner of the State 53
Dancing Under the Moon (with or without You) 56
NYK ROBERTSON
Black Satin Dress 57
MAUREEN BRADY
Adrienne Rich: Friendship Doubles My Universe 60
TRICIA ASKLAR
After Marriage 79
T. STORES
Love Theory #7 81
KAT MCALLISTER BLACK
The Wreck and the Butterfly Girl 100
RONNA MAGY
Echoes 102
DINAH DIETRICH
Vortex 104
DIANE FURTNEY
Jeredith 105
Sailing to Mytilene 107
MICHELLE LYNNE KOSILEK
Mutagenic Diaspora 113

RED WASHBURN
    Enjera 116
JANINE MERCER
    Burial Writes: Coming of Age in the Funeral Industry 118
HEATHER SEGGEL
    How to Bury Your Life at Sea: A Ritual 129
APRIL JO MURPHY
    Partners 131
MAUREEN SEATON
    Chick Lit 144
    Absurd Fiction 145
    Metafiction 146
CAROL ANNE DOUGLAS
    Old Lesbians Organizing for Change 25th Anniversary
    Gathering 147

    Book Reviews 149
    Contributors 159
    Advertisements 167

NOTES FOR A MAGAZINE

2015 marks *Sinister Wisdom's* 39th year of publishing. Hard to believe how time passes. The very first issue of Sinister Wisdom was born on July 4, 1976, the bicentennial of the United States; editors and publishers Catherine Nicholson and Harriet Desmoines delighted in that radical subversion of the holiday. A number of other exciting things happened in 1976: the Michigan Womyn's Music Festival started, Olivia Records released an LP of Pat Parker and Judy Grahn's poetry titled "Where Would I Be Without You?," feminists organized the first Take Back The Night Marches to stop violence against women, Naiad Books published Jeannette Foster's translation of Renee Vivien's *A Woman Appeared to Me*. It was an exciting year. As you can imagine, I am cooking up some wonderful issues and activities to celebrate our 40th year of publishing. More on those later. Meanwhile, this issue of *Sinister Wisdom, Sinister Wisdom 95: Reconciliation* is chock-full of great writing to sustain and nourish you. *Sinister Wisdom 95: Reconciliation* kicks off another fantastic year of lesbian-feminist publishing.

In these pages, you'll find a new short story by Annmarie Monahan, author of the incredible lesbian-feminist novel *Three* (if you haven't read it, rush to get a copy now!); fiction by T. Stores, Janine Mercer, and April Jo Murphy; memoir by Maureen Brady about Adrienne Rich; poetry by Maureen Seaton, Diane Furtney, Nyk Robertson—and many others; and a true-life caper story by a pack of lesbians who drove across the country in 1971 on the Dyke Outlaw Road Trip. It is a pleasure to bring all of these writers together within the pages of *Sinister Wisdom*.

When I first started as an editor of *Sinister Wisdom*, my sole focus was on keeping *Sinister Wisdom* alive. I wanted the journal to survive; I wanted the journal to live to carry the dreams and ideas of lesbians into the future. Today, almost five years later, I still am aware of the precarious nature of all lesbian-feminist projects (I do not think that we can ever believe our work and our institutions will last forever, that we can ever become complacent about the things that we value), but I feel more assured about the journal's survival and about my role as editor. In this issue, you will see evidence of that assurance in the form of some provocations, some work that is challenging, even risky. Work that I think is important published to a community that I love and cherish and that I believe can withstand the provocations, conflicts, challenges, and risks of the moment. As always, I look forward to your feedback—thoughtful and candid.

Thank you to everyone who contributed to *Sinister Wisdom* during our fall fundraising campaign. Your support of *Sinister Wisdom* and commitment to its present and future is humbling. A full list of donors to *Sinister Wisdom* from the fall fundraising campaign will be in our summer issue, *Sinister Wisdom 97*. This spring, in April and May, I will conduct a subscriber campaign like last year. The goal is simple: to add thirty-nine new subscribers to celebrate *Sinister Wisdom's* 39th year of publishing great lesbian-feminist literary and artistic work. I hope you will think about friends, colleagues, and compatriots who should subscribe to *Sinister Wisdom* but are not currently. April and May of 2015 is a great time to take out a subscription—or give a gift subscription to a friend to discover the journal. As always, it is an extraordinary pleasure to edit and publish *Sinister Wisdom*. I hope that I am nurturing the flame in ways that allow us all to see and think and understand our lives as lesbians with more light, more truth, and more passion. I cannot wait for you to read this fantastic issue of *Sinister Wisdom* and the other issues coming in 2015. There is much to celebrate about lesbian life and imagination today. May some of your celebrations happen within these pages.

In sisterhood,
Julie R. Enszer, PhD
January 2015

AGNES

Annemarie Monahan

Four thousand. Maybe five. I've never been at a Take Back the Night rally so big. Reagan's started his second term and the country's sliding rightward, but this is Minnesota, the only state to have voted Democrat. Masses of women press Loring Park, roaring for speaker after speaker.

I help someone tie a red armband over her sleeve. Women are tearing strips from rolls of fabric and handing them out. Red for a survivor of rape or sexual abuse, green for a survivor of battering, lavender for a lesbian. "Increase lesbian visibility," urges a woman with a crew cut as she thrusts one toward me. "We're the backbone of this movement." And we are. Everywhere I look, there's a stranger with a lavender armband. I've only been in Minneapolis a month. I know no one in town but my pharmacy school classmates, who talk about nothing but exams and beer.

The windows across the road rattle and buzz with the noise. The park is ours. The night is ours. We cannot fail. Together, we can end violence against women.

"Now, into the streets! Take Back the Night!" shouts the woman onstage.

Hooting, we surge from the park toward Hennepin Avenue.

We march to the strip clubs, the topless bars. "Women are not for sale! Women are not for sale!" We howl at a porn theater showing a snuff film. "Murderers!" We raise our fists at the red glare of a massage parlor, known to have women trafficked from Laos. "Free the women! Let them out!" then "Shame! Shame!" as a few white guys emerge from the back like disturbed vermin. A deafening cheer rises as they run.

At the intersection of Third Street, women are dropping folded paper into a smoking cauldron. "Write down your abusers' names," cries a short dyke in a witch hat. "We ask the Great Mother to hear us!"

"No fire! They burned the witches! Bad energy!" someone scolds.

"You fight fire with fire," says a woman with Lesbian Haircut Number Five. The determination on her face somehow makes it not a cliché.

"That's right," I say.

"It's not a hex," the short dyke declares. "It's a hold harmless spell. So it's good energy."

"What's a hold harmless spell?" asks the fire-lover.

Nobody answers, so I do. "It's witchcraft to stop an abuser by any means necessary. So if he magically develops a conscience, great. If he gets hit by a truck, well, that's fine, too."

She squints at me, intrigued yet skeptical. "Do you think it really works?"

"Well, no. Not really," I admit. "But it can't hurt, can it?"

"But I thought hurting was an option," she says, a little confused.

"Oh, shit, right. I guess we'll just have to sing 'Kumbaya,' then." I can't help smirking a bit, and then we're both laughing.

"Hey, my name's Agnes." She puts out her hand.

"Liz."

Talking, we rejoin the march. She's originally from way North ("you know, the Iron Range, like Bob Dylan"), has a thing for geology, drives a city bus, and knows every neighborhood and building in Minneapolis/St. Paul. "Have you noticed the dolomitic limestone facades downtown?" She's joined some group called WAMM. "Women Against Military Madness. They wouldn't approve back home. They're still boasting their ore won the World Wars. You'd never know they named a town after Eugene Debs up there." She's quirky. Smart, if a bit literal. We talk for two miles. I try to explain some of the alternative culture sights—the trash-lid drummers, the giant puppets, the interpretive dancers. Agnes takes it all in, bewildered but willing.

The multitude churns into a more narrow street. Swept and separated, then pushed back together, we're on the other side of each other now. Agnes glances at my armband and stops as abruptly as if she's hit the ground after falling from a cliff.

"But...," she yelps. "You're a lesbian!"

I double-take so hard that I hear my neck pop.

"Err, yes." Aren't you?

The crowd sluices around us as we gawk at each other. Agnes is literally panting in mortification. She grabs my arm in panic, and then, looking down, snatches her hand back as if I've flashed my fangs.

"I'm so sorry," she wails. "But I was a nun seventeen years. Lesbianism..." she says the word gingerly, like it has sharp edges, "...was so forbidden. Unthinkable. Even particular friendship was such a taboo. I don't want you to think I'm a bigot. I don't want you to think I don't accept you. I..."

Whoa. I wave her apologies away. "It's fine." I take a more careful look at her. She's fully gray around the temples, much older than my twenty-three. The haircut shows off her Kennedy forehead, and her blue Metropolitan Transit Authority sweater vest matches her eyes. No, it's not Lesbian Haircut Number Five after all; it's Nun Haircut Number One. Not like there's a big difference. And not like there's a Nun Haircut Number Two. Still, if she's not gay, neither am I. "Okay, tell the truth now. You used to sing 'Kumbaya' all the time."

She stares at me, face stiff.

"C'mon," I coax. "At folk Mass?" I pantomime strumming a guitar.

She starts. "There was no singing. We were a silent order."

A silent order! Goddess, the poor thing. No wonder she's so green.

"Someone's too worried, my Looord..." I croon, grinning at her.

After a fraught pause, comprehension creeps across her face. She grins back.

We talk all the way to the end, Bryant Square Park, then lose each other in the tumult. After too many folky white girls and righteous noise bands, I decide it's time to go. I'm too broke to own a car, so I catch the #21 bus, east, to the crappiest part of town. Home.

I unlock the door, humming.

"The world changed yet?" my roommate snorts from the couch. She's shirtless, as usual. Her breasts sprawl down her chest, floppy as exhausted puppies.

I refuse to be brought down. "Getting there."

Done with the conversation, Larsen flicks a seed out of her stash. Only her mother calls her by her first name, Missy. She has the manners and the moustache of a fifteen-year-old boy. I'd had four days to find somewhere I could afford. When I found this place, cheap and with a lesbian roommate, I grabbed it. It never occurred to me that not every lesbian was a feminist.

Lying in bed, I think about Agnes. Amazing, the people you meet in Lesbian Nation. Or Should-Be-Lesbian Nation.

By morning, I've forgotten about her.

II

Hey, I know that woman!

"Agnes? What are you doing here?" I stage-whisper across the school library. Untangling myself from a knot of classmates, I make my way toward her.

She looks up, oddly pink in surprise. "Oh!" she says. "That's right, you're a student here." She indicates her armload of books. "I had some research to do. Some medical research. Pharmaceutical research." She frowns at the floor.

"Well, nice to see you again. Did you find what you need?"

"Oh, yes." She looks from the wall to the copy machine to the periodicals, but not at me. She's busy and I'm interrupting her. "You know, you never gave me your number last month."

"You want it? Okay." I tear a sheet of paper from my notebook and scrawl on it.

She glances at the exchange. "Seven-two-four. South Minneapolis."

"Right. Well, I'll let you get back to your research. Biochem starts in ten minutes. If you need help finding something else, ask the librarian with the big earrings over there. She's really nice."

She nods and turns back to the stack with a strangely gruff motion, dismissing me.

She calls the next night. She's not distant anymore. She's giddy as a kid unwrapping a bicycle-big box. I learn that she's forty, has driven for the MTA for six years, and lives with two cats, Hélène and Mister Mango. She dances from topic to topic, question to question. Did I know there'd been a murder on my block the summer before last? If I stood on my porch and looked left to 35W, I could see where the road cuts through a layer of shale, exposing St. Peter Sandstone underneath. I should go have a look. Why did I pick Minnesota for school?

"That reminds me," I jump in, wishing she'd say more about herself. "What were you researching at the library? I can order journal articles if you need the most up-to-date information."

"Oh, some medication my doctor recommended. Basic side effects. You know," she mumbles. "Nothing fancy."

She obviously doesn't want to talk about her health. I won't pry. It's rude.

"So pharmacy students do cadaver dissection?" she continues. "That's so interesting."

Agnes seems determined to make up for seventeen years of silence. She calls me several times a week, and would talk all night if I didn't beg off to study. She wants to know everything about me, but doesn't volunteer many details about herself. I have to press her.

"So, why exactly did you leave the convent?" I ask one day.

Something in the quiet tells me to back off.

"Sorry. Don't mean to get too personal."

"Oh, no. No, it's okay," she sighs. "A lot of women left religious life after Vatican II. My order was just so insular it took me longer to be affected."

"So you left because of the reforms."

"That was the beginning." She hesitates again. "I'd expressed some unorthodox opinions, and my superiors suggested I leave because of my health. Their excuse for getting rid of me."

"Your health?"

"Yes," she snaps. Personal disclosure over. "When did you leave the church?"

She switches topics suddenly. "Tell me about your first lover." She's breathless with her own daring.

Oh, honey, you are so coming out. "I loved her very much." I did, even though she was a drunk and an asshole. But no need to disillusion you with that.

"Were you soul mates? Was it love at first sight?"

I laugh. "I don't believe in love at first sight." Or souls.

"You don't?" Almost belligerent.

"It's just not realistic. You can't love a stranger. You don't know them." Sheesh, you'd think she would've gotten over any silly romantic ideas by her age.

"You don't think you can just know?" she demands. "You wouldn't listen to that voice speaking to you? A divine voice? When it spoke to you and you knew?" Her pitch rises dangerously.

I have no idea what to say. "I guess so, Agnes," I murmur.

"Could I take you to brunch?" she asks. "This weekend?"

"That would be great. I'm so sick of rice and lentils. But midterms are coming up—maybe when they're over? The weekend after next?"

"Sunday the ninth? Is eleven okay? I'll pick you up."

Is this a date? Like a date, date? I find myself liking the idea. She's a bit strange, but I've always been drawn to smart, strange women. Plus she's a lot older. I've pursued older women—unsuccessfully—but this one is pursuing me. In her own way. I think. And, I have to admit it, I'm lonely. I've been too consumed by school to find new friends. "Okay. What bus stop?"

She pauses. "With my car."

Why is she so concrete sometimes? I laugh. Catching on, she does, too.

After we make the brunch date, she calls every night. I still enjoy our conversations, but it's almost impossible to get her off the phone.

"Eleven more days!" she cries merrily. "How's the studying?"

"Okay, I guess. But, Agnes, I'm sorry, I have to get back to it..."

"Oh, of course. Okay, well, good luck! Talk to you tomorrow!"

Funny, overexcited thing. But it's cute.

"Eight days. Where were you last night?" Her tone has an edge I've never heard from her before.

"At the lab. It's midterms."

"Out with your lover," she spits.

I blink. "Huh? I don't have a girlfriend, Agnes. All I do is study."

She pauses. "Just kidding!" She laughs loudly. "So I was doing some reading about the settlement of St. Paul, and if you can believe it, the city was first named 'Pig's Eye'..."

I don't have time to make sense of it later. I have another exam the next morning.

"Hello?"

"Three days!"

"Tomorrow! It's tomorrow!"

Agnes knocks twenty minutes early. Still in my room, I hear my roommate heave herself up from the couch.

"Hey, your friend's here," she yells as I come into the living room. Thank God she's wearing a shirt. She sits back down with a heavy grunt and turns up the TV.

"Hi," says Agnes. She holds out a tin of Bag Balm and quart of eggnog, both wrapped with silver ribbon.

Gifts? On a first date? It's too much. Over-intimate. But I thank her. "That's really nice of you. Umm, did I tell you I love eggnog?"

"No. I just knew." She smiles and looks down, bashful. "The Bag Balm is for your hands. After dissection lab. To keep them soft."

Larsen snickers.

I will not blush, I will not blush. "So thoughtful. Hold on a sec, I'll put the eggnog in the fridge and we can go." Ignore my roommate. She's not my friend, okay?"

Larsen doesn't look up from MTV when we leave. Eyes fixed on Lisa Lisa's cleavage, she's sealing her rolling paper with broad, slow strokes of her tongue.

We drive to a supermarket in some suburb. A very strange supermarket. It has chandeliers and carpet in the aisles. The carts make no noise as coiffed old ladies push them around the artful displays. She leads me to the back, to an attached restaurant. After the hostess hands us menus, we're seated at a pleather booth, high-backed and private.

I've never seen anybody so agitated. Agnes stares at me like she can't believe I'm really there. She jumps from topic to topic, trembling like she's had an entire plantation's worth of coffee. No, like a woman poised at the open door of a plane, thrilled by the rush of Earth beneath her. She hasn't touched her food.

"You know why I was in that library, don't you?" She leans forward, her face joyous as someone confiding a miracle. "I had to find you. And I did."

She sits back, smiling. "It didn't matter how angry I was. I thought you'd lied to me about living in South Minneapolis. I thought you lied to me about your name. I couldn't find you anywhere. You weren't in the book. Did you know there's an Elizabeth Russo in White Bear Lake? She always insisted she wasn't you, though. I was so, so angry." She jabs her fork into her walleye hot dish.

"I didn't lie to you," I gulp. "The phone's under my roommate's name."

"I understand that now. I understood after I saw you in the library. You hadn't lied to me after all. You were a student there, just like you said." Is that a dawn lighting her face, or an approaching wildfire? "And you gave me your number. You had to see me, too. But I already knew you did. I've known since the rally. A voice came that night. They always let me know."

Speechless, I push my wild rice omelet away.

"Ever since we met..." she takes a breath, squeezing her eyes shut, "'... I am come into my garden, my sister, my spouse: I have gathered my myrrh with my spice; I have eaten my honeycomb with my honey; I have drunk my wine with my milk.'" She looks up again. "I can tell you now. Every night I dream of you..." her gaze falls to my breasts "...giving me suck."

Before that moment, if anyone had asked, I might have said it'd be hot to have an ex-nun talk Song of Solomon dirty to me. And I would've been mistaken. Embarrassingly, appallingly mistaken. I'm freaking out. My tongue sticks to the roof of my mouth like a communion wafer.

But hold it. This can't be personal. It's too intense to be about me. This is years of longing exploding, the eruption of a long-tamped volcano. I just happen to be caught too near the vent.

"Oh God, I'm flattered. I've never been so flattered in my life. But, Agnes, listen, you're not in love with me. You can't be."

The light in her face fades. She sits, still as a darkened room.

"I'm not saying you can't be a lesbian. I bet if you think about it, you've been in love with women before. But we don't know each other that well. And...well...aren't I the first out lesbian you've ever met? Maybe it's not me? Maybe you've been waiting to come out for years and I'm the dyke in front of you?"

The muscles of her jaw tighten.

"I'm really sorry, I don't want to hurt you. But I don't want to steer you wrong. I don't think this is about me. I think this is about women."

She stands up.

"No, please. I'm sorry. This is awful. But please just listen for..."

Agnes throws some cash on the table and stomps away. I trot after her. I have no other way to get home. Only a five in my pocket, too poor for credit cards, far beyond any bus route. I don't even know what suburb we're in. I'm trapped.

We're out of the parking lot before I get my belt on. We drive back to the edge of the city. And drive, and drive. Lake of the Isles Parkway, Lake Calhoun Parkway, Lake Harriet Parkway, Lake Calhoun Parkway, Lake of the Isles Parkway... We're going around in circles.

"Agnes, please take me home."

"I'll take you home all right," she leers.

"No! I mean, no. Bring me back to my apartment. And leave me there. Alone."

She slowly turns to face me, polar-pale in rage. The blue ice of her eyes cracks into a million crevasses. She shoves her foot down on the gas. The engine shrieks.

"Come on. Stop."

She ignores me. The speedometer slides past forty...fifty...

"Agnes, please!"

We flash past a twenty-five mph sign at fifty-four.

"There's rope in the attic," she mutters, more to herself than me. "More than enough, even with the noose."

I brace my feet against the floor, yanked from side to side as we take the curves. My elbow smacks the door with every new twist. Yuppie runners and their dogs look up in alarm as we blast by.

"The garage is better than the basement. More room to drop."

"There's no reason to hang yourself! You can have a girlfriend. This isn't about me!"

"Stop saying that!" she screams.

"Okay, okay." Closing my eyes, I reconsider my approach. "Look, Agnes, coming out is tough. I understand that. There's a book you might like. It's called *Lesbian Nuns*. And have you ever thought about talking to a therapist?"

"I already have one of those. She's useless. Her and those prescriptions."

I fight to keep my voice even. "Prescriptions?"

She spits a list. Even as first-year student, I recognize two of them as antipsychotics. Oh, shit. Shit! The mysterious matchmaking voice. The being asked to leave the convent for health reasons. Why am I so dense? Now what do I do?

Inspiration jolts me like a shot of epinephrine.

"Would you like some help? Maybe I can make your therapist understand. You know, understand what you're going through. Do you want me to talk to her?"

The speedometer wavers and falls to forty-five.

"Yes, I'll talk to her. She'll listen. What's her name?"

She tells me. Thirty-two mph. She turns off Lake Calhoun Parkway.

"Take me back and I'll call her," I urge. Please, please.

My hand's already on the latch as we pull up outside my place. We meet eyes for the first time in five miles. Agnes shuts off the engine and leans in, as if she's going to kiss me. Wriggling away from her, I jump out of the car.

"Uh, thanks for brunch," I call, waving idiotically. I flee up the sidewalk.

I run through the living room—past my roommate, ear-deep in a bong—and into my room. I lock myself in, and the bang of the bolt rings through the apartment.

After a moment of surprised silence, Larsen's outside my door.

"Didn't get laid?" Still not exhaling as she laughs, she ends up coughing.

The phone book listings blur as I search. How can this city possibly support thirty pages of therapists? Not finding Agnes's,

I flip into the White Pages. Maybe the practice has an answering service. They'll call her. This is an emergency.

My God, there's a home number. I hesitate, but Agnes could be knotting that rope as I stand here. I dial with sweating hands.

She answers. A miracle. "Cynthia Bergstrom."

"I'm really worried about Agnes Dey," I blurt.

She sighs. "Aren't we all?"

Of course she can't tell me anything. But she does listen, tells me not to worry, then thanks me for my concern.

But how could I not worry?

The next three nights, I check the paper for news of a suicide. Nothing.

On the fourth night, the phone rings. Larsen answers. "Snow bunnies. How can we hump you?" She scowls and shoves the phone at me. "It's your girlfriend."

"Agnes!" She's not dead.

"You can't just pretend!" she howls.

Pretend? Never mind, it doesn't have to make sense. "I'm glad you're all right," I get out.

"What do you care? You use me and toss me aside! Maybe it's nothing to you, but I've never been with anybody else, do you understand me? Never!" Her fury frays into sobs.

"But..." She's crying so hard that I don't pursue it. "I talked to your therapist. Did she..."

"She says you're not worth dying over," she boils.

"She's right. I'm not."

She hisses and hangs up.

She calls every night. I'm relieved to know she's not dead. I can bear with this until it burns itself out. And it seems to. After a week, she's decided that we can be friends despite my evil, using ways. When I decline to get together so I can apologize, her reproaches and screaming get louder and less intelligible. But she hasn't mentioned hurting herself since the first call. She'll be okay. After another week, I tell my roommate that I'm not taking any more calls from Agnes.

"Bargain Meat, eat it or beat it... No, she's not here." Larsen glares at me. "Wanna leave a... Fuck!" She hurls the phone off the couch. "Your girlfriend again," she growls. "Does she think I won't know who keeps hanging up? Two weeks! I'm sick of her shit. Talk to her and make her stop."

The next night, Larsen and I are having yet another chat about the heat bill.

"I don't care. Sixty-five is just too damn cold."

"Maybe if you kept your shirt on, you'd stay warm enough. And maybe you should drink hot coffee instead of all my eggnog. I can't—"

The phone rings, and we freeze. We both know who it is. Larsen picks up and slings the receiver into my lap. "Tell her to bring more eggnog," she grunts.

I drag the phone into my room and teeter on the edge of my desk. "Agnes, we have to talk."

She's sobbing too angrily to say anything.

"Agnes, I'm not a good friend to you."

"No, you're not," she finally gets out.

"Listen to you. That's how upset I make you."

"Yes," she weeps. "It's terrible."

"It's not fair, is it?"

No answer.

"It's not fair, is it? Is that how friends make you feel, Agnes?"

"No. You're a terrible friend," she whimpers.

She's stopped crying. This can't really work, can it?

"I've been selfish," I sigh. "It's not right for me to hold onto you when I make you this upset."

"Selfish. It's not right," she echoes, crying again.

"So I think I should be brave and end this friendship. I'm no good for you, Agnes." I hold my breath.

She doesn't hesitate. "You're no good for me. You're just no good. You're a terrible, terrible friend!"

"Then this is goodbye, Agnes. Goodbye."

"Goodbye," she wails.

She hangs up.

I place the receiver on its cradle gently, as if too sudden a motion might disturb the fragile peace. No way that's the end. She'll decide to forgive me and give me another chance.

But I don't hear from her again.

III

Halfway through our second spring, our workloads ease enough that we don't study every weekend anymore. One Monday morning, my pathologically Minnesotan classmate Karen joins me in the coffee line. She's wearing the closest to a smirk I've ever seen her.

"I met one of your exes Friday night."

One of my what? My nearest ex is 1200 miles away. I've only started seeing someone in town a few months ago. "Who?" Nobody from back East had called about a visit.

"Agnes Dey." She smiles at the shock on my face. "Guess you remember her. Bad breakup, eh?"

"No. No, I mean... Agnes... she's..."

"Yah, she was pretty surprised, too. It was funny. Julie and I went to Heck Bar..."

Hell Bar is the only lesbian bar in The Cities. At least everyone calls it that. It's been named Ladies' Night, Lesdames, Peg's Panic, Our Kind—ever-changing owners, same red-walled, hell-hot dive.

"...and we bumped into her friend Ginny and her new girlfriend. Ginny and Julie went to dance, so I was sitting talking with the girl, and for sure, she seemed pretty smart and interesting. She asked me what I do. When I told her, she jumped up all upset and walked away. Just like that. I thought, uff da, does she hate pharmacists or something? But she came back in a while. Said she was really sorry, but she'd had a really bad experience with a pharm student. Maybe I knew her. Liz Russo? I said, 'Hey, sure, I know Liz. She's in my year.' And she got up and tromped off again!" Karen shakes her head, laughing.

A little strangling sound escapes my throat and she interprets it as laughing along.

"Oh, for strange, you bet. So, she came back again and said sorry, it's just that you really gave her the business." She pokes me. "You Casanova. Love 'er and leave 'er, eh?" Her light tone can't disguise the dismay in her eyes.

Why, why did I ever tell any of my classmates stories of how wild I was in college?

"She's crazy. This is crazy. She's not my ex." I tell her the whole story. Take Back the Night. The library. Brunch. When I get to the phone calls, she interrupts.

"Ya, well, you sure made an impression on her!" Something in her face rolls shut.

It's too much for Karen. It's bizarre. It's unpleasant. It's kind of perverted. And nice, lefse-bland lesbians with Holly Near hair will always believe that truth lies exactly halfway between two stories, however incompatible. I must have done something outrageous. After all, hadn't I pushed my way through my lab partners to hemisect our cadaver's penis, halves curling under my eager scalpel like an over-boiled hot dog? Everybody knew that. (Okay, I did volunteer, but only after I got tired of everyone freaking out and clutching their groins. Not even the women had the guts to start the assignment. And okay, I never poured weed killer on the rumors that grew into an impenetrable thicket around the truth. Better to get called a castrating bitch behind my back than a "purple tofu eater" like all the other lesbians.) Clearly, I was capable of anything.

She frowns at her shoes a long moment, then brightens. "Heckuva Twins game last night, eh?"

IV

I graduate two years later. A month before I move back East, I board a #34 bus and flash my pass at... Agnes. We gape at each other.

"Sit down," she finally growls.

"Agnes...," I say.

"Sit DOWN," she shouts. People stare.

I sit down.

Snarling, she shoves the bus into gear and we rocket from the curb.

We grind down Cedar Avenue. Agnes glowers at me in her passenger-view mirror, barely glancing at the road. An indignant murmur rises from the crowd like a bad smell. Look how angry the driver is. What did that girl do? Troublemaker. Get off the bus! To my left, an elderly woman watches me, lips pursed, as she stabs her knitting. The young punk across the aisle, his hair a much darker blue, solidarity-scowls at me over an issue of *The Daily Worker*. The barbell through his eyebrow points at my chest like an accusing finger.

I stand up and pull the stop-request cord. We're half a mile from my apartment—close enough to walk, and I don't want Agnes to know where I live, anyway.

We hiss to a stop at Lake Street. I make my way toward the front of the bus, every eye a prod in my back. As I near Agnes, she opens the door and pointedly looks away, out her window. I exit, onto the sidewalk and into my Agnes-free future.

A FEMINIST KIND OF SEX

Gizelle S.

1.
her name: an acquired taste
and a power
too often refracted
vilified before its own sight
fucked into hiding
by a constructed shame
lips silenced
sewed shut.

her name: choked on by novice voices
spat out by the oppressive tongues
that fetishize
that demonize
that infantilize
the strength within her walls

must own it.   must subdue it.
it is   what   it is.

it
is colonial letters
that replace her native name.

2.
my mouth tenders refuge
from blasphemy
from vulgar, hollow words
and speaks her truth with an attentive tongue.

indebted to her first letter,
my voice's tenant,
i have permission to finally
trust
hear my own depth.
i swallow her salty tears
with each blunt grunt exorcized from
spots marked by other letters
and verify mine
and her own value
as virgin and vagabond, vocally unashamed.

IN EXILE

Gizelle S.

i suckled on Reggae's breasts
obedient to the heartbeat of a rhythm
that "jus' feel right."

my tongue tickled Patois' pleasure centers,
tasting her forbidden phrases as they sat side-saddle on my lips
but hidden from Mummy, whose Holy Water lay
neatly in her bosom
between her tithe and antidepressants
ready to do god's bidding.

I synched my cycles with the Blue Mountains' visiting moon,
a proposition affirmed the first night she swung
atop Missa Grant's leering coconut tree.
we bled together each month
naively convinced that
the red and the dead by our feet
both fell from us.

but skies reflect the seas' conformity.
illegal rainbows brought to vigilant justice
tell me to run
to keep my colors
before waves of sameness between this land and that
suck my green and gold
leaving only black, me,
on a foreign concrete that misunderstands my hellos
and cries for the sun,
but allows me to love ripening rains
and other bodies like,
yet unlike
my own.

THE FIRST SIN

Gizelle S.

our lips synched in unlawful union
just outside the closet
where Auntie kept her church shoes
down the deaf hill
as indignant hallelujahs faded
between the blades of obedient grass
that grew as in Genesis –
their place in heaven more secure than ours.

there, I first bit Apple,
the earth's own fruit, shined
to corrupt salvation –
her smile summoned heat
from hell; our shared breath
unlearned from my mind
lessons of righteousness delivered Sundays before.

the sun lowered its head earlier than usual
and the moon used its monthly excuse that day:
neatly prepared alibis for the day
of judgment when Jesus
and the Devil
would ask if they saw me
brushing away biblical "nos"
and willingly give myself to the fire
as an Eve on the edge of Eden.

1971 DYKE OUTLAW ROAD TRIP

Roberta Arnold, Phyllis Bloom, Reeni Goldin, M. Patricia Yasin Orenda Thíe ie ka:ken

We are four of many lesbian revolutionaries who had met in the 1970s, four in the chorus of voices heralding a new way of being women in the world. I know less about who we were in terms of where we came from, and I know more about how we were united: Reeni, Buffy, now going by her Mohawk name: Orenda Thíe ie Ka:ken, Phyllis, and me, Berta. I think Reeni and Phyllis were in their twenties, Buffy was nineteen, and I was eighteen. What mattered most to us was that we were together in this fight—we believed in the revolution of women loving women—against a patriarchy that was classist, racist, and sexist. We were making our own world, a place of freedom for all women and the oppressed. We met through the Fifth Street Building Takeover in New York City. Now, over forty years later, we are retelling our stories of that time.

REENI: We were outlaws. We had consciousness. It was a great time to come out and be alive.

BERTA: I was born for the women's movement. I was made stronger by its rising. Patriarchy overshadowed everything back then: the way we lived, the way we thought, the air we breathed. We were reclaiming life, believing in ourselves, believing we were right.

PHYL: Absolutism is interesting! We were passionate, united, community-centric, as women, lesbians, and revolutionaries, and we were also righteous. The righteousness brought fervor and pushed us toward change we saw as imperative, but on reflecting back, it also, as it does globally, created separations and divisions that meant the movement had ultimately changed to something else. But at the time we were part of an exuberant and strong force toward liberation. And that was a totally important part of the process, and fantastic for those of us who were involved in it.

BUFFY: I remember the purity of feelings...the unfiltered gut response...still based on the innocence all injustice could be stopped. When definitions start to get made it takes the sacredness out, the gut level of what we would be. We were... the dog soldiers, the ones who were the front guards, the pathfinders, and the renegades.

* * *

This was the advent of lesbian feminism. This was our fight. We believed no woman would be left out. No sister would be unheard. We were creating definitions as we went along. Most of our slogans rose from actions and were not ours alone.

The Personal Is Political. Women Take Back the Night. Women Belong in the House and the Senate. A Woman Without a Man Is Like a Fish Without a Bicycle. Women United Cannot Be Defeated. Smash Patriarchy! Women Uprising! Lesbians Unite!

Our message was about being visible, stopping rape and attack, being independent of men, claiming our rightful worth, being united as women—rising up from positions dividing us, to being united on a single front. We weren't afraid to name our oppressor. His name was man.[1]

As far as I know, the only slogan attributed to one person was from a poem by Judy Grahn in her poetry collection *The Work of a Common Woman: The Collected Poetry of Judy Grahn 1964–1977.*

---

[1] "Oppression is something that one group of people commits against another group specifically because of a 'threatening' characteristic shared by the latter group—skin color or sex or age, etc."—from the article "Goodbye to All That" by Robin Morgan, printed on the takeover of *Rat* (1970); reprinted in *Going Too Far: The Personal Chronicles of a Feminist* (New York: Vintage, 1978).

A common woman is
As common as a common loaf of bread —
AND WILL RISE.[2]

"An army of lovers shall not fail" was said to have been introduced by Jill Johnston, writer for *The Village Voice* at the time. These words were originally attributed to Plato and male warriors, but we co-opted the slogan as our own. In 1974, Rita Mae Brown made this the last line of her poem in "Sappho's Reply."[3]

I was aligned with the rising of all my sisters across the board. My mother, June Arnold, steered me to the revolution; she believed in rocking the boat. In 1970, my mother embraced the lesbian feminist movement and so did I. We were standing side by side then—coming out in the same world at the same time. As women's voices were heard, I became keenly aware of the deep woundings amongst us, especially in issues of class and race. The anger and outrage shared throughout our learning worked to challenge the political frameworks and create shared humanity. Many of us delved into race and class oppression. We examined our racist attitudes and practices as pointed out to us by women of color, and we listened. We held each other and bore witness to our broken hearts. I disagree with what is written about the second wave—predominantly being projected as a group of self-interested white middle-class women as the media now suggests; this is just a falsehood. Working class and women of color were making their voices heard. In the beginning we were uniting around the fact that all women were creating a new social order. The initial circle grew and split into smaller circles as we continued opening outward.

2 Judy Grahn, "The common woman," *The Work of a Common Woman: The Collected Poetry of Judy Grahn 1964–1977* (Oakland, CA: Diana Press, 1978); Judy Grahn, "A woman is talking to death," *The Work of a Common Woman: The Collected Work of Judy Grahn 1964–1977* (Trumansburg, NY: Crossing Press, 1978).
3 Rita Mae Brown, "Sappho's Reply," *The Hand That Cradles the Rock* (New York: New York University Press, 1974, first print).

I joined the lesbian feminist culture made up of all the different aspects of us. Perhaps the issue of seeing men as the oppressor was too big, too woven into the fabric of most women's lives, to be a fight we could win, but fighting against the domination of the racist white patriarchy was the common denominator of our struggle. We heard our black sisters when delineating a three-tier history of oppression being black, working class, and female.[4] At first, the NBFO (National Black Feminist Organization) was embracing feminism and relegating top priorities to race and class. Later, the Combahee River Collective was embracing lesbian feminism, race, and class.[5] Then the Iowa City Collective also began embracing lesbian feminism and examining conversations of race and class. The demand to have the lesbian issue stand beside abortion and women's health in NOW (National Organization for Women) caused turmoil and thus came Lavender Menace—the Redstockings and Radicalesbians were already buzzing hives of political activity. How many groups were there? And not just in the US but across the globe? So many groups were springing up. We were forming tribes, getting ourselves stronger and ready— we were rising up.

Perhaps why we didn't succeed in the unification of our movement had less to do with divisions and infighting and more to do with outside forces. Also during this time (early 1970s), an article published on *The New York Times* stated that the fbi was infiltrating the women's movement in an effort to destroy its power. Whether

---

4   Barbara Smith, Response to Adrienne Rich's "Notes for a Magazine: What Does Separatism Mean?" *Sinister Wisdom* 20, 1982.

5   "The National Black Feminist Organization was founded in 1973 in New York by Margaret Sloan-Hunter and others. In 1975, Barbara Smith, Beverly Smith, Cheryl L. Clarke, Akasha Gloria Hull, and other female activists established the Combahee River Collective—named after a Harriet Tubman guerrilla action in 1863 freeing multitudes of slaves... The only military campaign in American history planned and led by a woman." The Combahee River Collective, "A Black Feminist Statement." In Cherrie Moraga and Gloria Anzaldua (eds.). *This Bridge Called My Back: Writings by Radical Women of Color* (Watertown, MA: Persephone Press, 1981), 211.

or not this was a major cause of our lessening ground swell, the infiltration undoubtedly contributed to unification breakdowns. We wrote "fbi" in lowercase letters instead of capitals to minimize the importance of their power over us, though at times we gave them too much power nevertheless, and made mistakes along the way.

REENI: I remember when the article in *Rat* came out about the lesbian fbi agent who had slept with so many lesbians. We picked three or four friends we knew we could trust and formed cells. Each woman in the cell was responsible for keeping track of others.

PHYL: I was working in the women's *Rat* collective when that story came out...before we took our trip...we had our own agent sitting in his car on our corner every day. I'd say that the *Rat* collective radicalized me and positively educated me almost more than anything else ever had.[6]

***

The political divisions and fbi infiltration did not stop us. As is the process of ongoing grassroots political struggles, we divided and regrouped, separating into smaller factions where powers were claimed and nourished; we moved forward. *The Woman-Identified Woman* by Radicalesbians came into being in 1970, identifying the rage of lesbians who had been ostracized—redefining what it meant to be a lesbian.[7] Women's anger toward other women, I felt then, as an offshoot of patriarchal rule—a roadblock built to keep us apart—and within our outlaw band, we fought to tear down

---

6   *Rat*, a subterranean newspaper on the Lower East Side, became a collective of radical women in 1970 and the name became "Women's LibeRATion." http://en.wikipedia.org/wiki/Rat_(newspaper)

7   Radicalesbians, *The Woman-Identified Woman* (Pittsburgh: Know, Inc., c. 1970). Now archived in Duke University: http://library.duke.edu/rubenstein/scriptorium/wlm/womid/

these walls. The vitriol rearing up amongst us would one day shine a spotlight on all the unheard voices. But at the time, I felt simply lucky, lucky for my mother saying, "The first love we all share, if we're one of the lucky ones, is woman-love." Love from a mother. Though I would soon know more deeply the different individual truths about our differences, at the time I chose to see all women through the eyes of love. Not only did I fall in love with so many of the women I came upon at that time, but I loved the idea of living only in a world of women. And this was happening not just with me but with many of us. Suddenly the world had changed, and there we were in the thick of it—visibly alive and in charge of our own stories. Everywhere we went, the world was vibrant. We were alive in nature: in woods, lakes, and women's private land; in word, action, and song. The world was rising up with us. We danced, took off our clothes, sang songs we had created, wrote poetry, and lived free from any eyes but our own. Images of us were being recorded: in sketches, paintings, photography, film, and word—all by us, for us. Part of our statement in bucking the system was about being visible in the public eye as well— as dykes out in the open; the word "dyke" was taken by us as a moniker for pride. While we were re-defining what it meant to be ourselves, we were redefining what it meant to be a lesbian. Splitting off into new-formed worlds, like bands of horses running wild and free, feeling our way, exacting our spirits—reflecting back on life's vision—in shining, liquid eyes. Sometimes we were combustible. Not just flammable; we were the flame.

Living Our Dreams as Lesbian Outlaws

JANUARY 1971: We met at the Fifth Street Women's Building Takeover: the squatting action an abandoned city-owned building on the Lower East Side. My mother, my sister, and me had been involved in squatting actions in the West Village— occupying apartments because greedy landlords were evicting rent-controlled tenants to raise the rent. While across town, over on the Lower East Side, in the Cooper Union Committee, Reeni and her mother, Frances Goldin, were involved in similar, planned, organized, and historic action.[8]

My mother, June Arnold,[9] met Reeni at the West Side Women's Center on Twenty-Second Street.

REENI: June and I both went to the file cabinet at the same time, and, as it turned out, we were both reaching for the same card: "Housing." We got to talking. I had a tremendous crush on June back then. She was so sophisticated, and I was a little in awe of her. I told June about the lack of women's resources on the Lower East Side.[10] I said we needed a women's resource center there.

---

8   From Frances Goldin's website: http://www.ittook50.com: "My family were Russian Jews who left to escape the pogroms and oppression. We lived in an area that was Christian, thirty-five hundred people, and nine Jews. When I was about eleven, I had very few friends, I was pretty isolated, but I had one friend who had a sister whom I couldn't stand, nor she me. And then somehow on the way home from school we got into a fight. Then a circle of boys surrounded the fight and they were yelling, 'Kill the Jew. Kill the Jew.' And when they said that, I went berserk. I went crazy. And I grabbed the child's ears and I was banging her head against the curb, and somebody who was on my back said, 'Frances, please stop, she has a heart condition.'

"And it was her sister who was trying to get me to stop killing her. And I looked up and on the porch of my house, which was a half a block away, I saw my father standing. And I kind of came to my senses and got up and staggered home. He took me inside and put me on his lap and rocked me. And I was beside myself that he had exposed me to that and didn't stop it. And he said, 'Girlie-Girlie,' which is his term of affection, 'this was your fight, not mine. You had to have this fight and you'll never have to fight again.' And at the time I didn't understand that, but it turned out to be true. People walked across the street when they'd see me coming. They'd turn around and go back to where they came from. So that was a turning point for me. I was as isolated as ever, but I never did have to fight again. Except I've been fighting all my life, but not that kind of fighting." Frances Goldin is a socialist activist and editor. She began the Goldin Literary Agency in NYC and also instrumental in the idea for the book *Imagine: Living in a Socialist USA*, edited by Francis Goldin, Debby Smith, and Michael Steven Smith.

9   June Fairfax Davis Arnold was the author of five novels, founder of Daughters, Inc., and instrumental planner in the Fifth Street Women's Building Takeover and the Women in Print Conference.

10   Lower East Side History: Cooper Union Committee: http://www.eastvillagearts.org/lower-eastside-history-cooper-square-committee-part-2-of-3/

BERTA: I remember your mom, Fran—a fighter like my mom, yet even more so. When I called to speak to you over at Cooper Square, I sometimes got Fran on the phone. Fran spoke to me like an equal. No matter how little experience or expertise I had, she listened to what I said—as if it mattered a lot. She made me feel important.

REENI: I was working at Cooper Square at Cooper Union. My mom had been fighting for tenant's rights there for many years. Cooper Union was a radical response to the city's urban renewal plan for undergoing gentrification. The city was going to demolish and evict low-income tenants to make trendy apartments for middle-class families. The Cooper Union Committee had a history of demonstrations in favor of tenant rights. They were organized and well-developed. The Cooper Union Committee was helping people keep their apartments. Housing was central to survival back then. Housing was about a place to survive and work, not about owning a home. I didn't understand about owning a home back then. I had a tiny two-room apartment for $37.95 per month. Well, it was really three rooms, but then they came and put a toilet in the third room, where the toilet had been down the hall—so there went that room. And a bathtub sat in the kitchen. So there was only one room to be in and that was the living room, which became my bedroom. I knew nothing about ownership of a home. There were no co-ops, or condos, back then. I thought a home was something you built from the ground up and then never left. The idea of selling your home was foreign to me. That was like a secondhand home. Who would want that? Plus, being a city kid from socialist parents, we were not ownership-oriented. We thought the city should provide housing and health care and help the majority of women, then, on welfare to survive. We understood that having a low-rent apartment was the key to survival.

***

Despite negotiations with the mayor's office and representative mouthpieces, the city shut down the plans for a women's resource center—the Fifth Street Women's Building Takeover lasted twelve days. But many alliances that were made during those days didn't die. The four of us bonded: Reeni, Buffy, Phyllis, and me—plus Phyllis' partner at the time, Jessie. Jessie met up with the rest of us after I had gone, but she was with us through Phyllis by phone calls. By that spring, we were meeting in the bedroom/living room of Reeni's apartment on the Lower East Side, talking of driving cross-country, stopping at women's centers and national parks, and meeting up with different women's groups along the way. Thus began our small band of lesbian outlaws, sprawled out in Reeni's apartment, probably smoking pot, dreaming up the idea of a cross-country road trip.

Beginning of Road Trip

BERTA: We left from the loft building where my mom lived, packing up the car the night before so we wouldn't have any drudge work just before we left. That morning, when we met at the car, I noticed the van windows partly open. Inside was empty. Everything we had piled up the night before was gone. Of course we were mad, but it was New York City so getting ripped off was part of life. And getting mad was about being who we were. We howled into the sky and raised our fists high in the air. As Reeni says, we had outlaw perspective. High on our powers, we got into the car and drove off toward the interstate. We began the cross-country drive in an old VW van that Reeni had spotted and bought for the trip. It was going to need some work, but Buffy, Reeni, and Phyllis had gone to the University of the Streets following Fifth Street, so they knew a thing or two about fixing cars.[11]

---

11 The University of the Streets in the East Village was founded in 1967, by Fred Good and Robert Theobald, with inspiration drawn from Hispanic gang members on the Lower East Side on teaching people in the streets to survive lawfully.

REENI: One of us painted a woman's symbol over the VW logo on the front of the van. It might have been Jessie. I remember we had a discussion about that. You know, on the front of the VW where they have the circle with the VW logo inside? We wanted to put our logo there. We talked about painting a lesbian symbol on the front, but we knew we were going into "enemy territory" so we decided not to do that. We talked about a woman's symbol with a rifle inside but decided that was too dangerous. A regular woman's symbol was too namby-pamby, so we finally decided to paint a black woman's symbol with a fist inside it (a popular symbol of the time).

PHYL: I learned how to change points and plugs and tires and do basic car maintenance at another revolutionary women's collective up in Windham, New York. I remember feeling thrilled to be in a VW bus because the bugs and busses were the cars we had all learned on for the most part. We studied survival skills and independence along with politics. The survival skills were some of the skills that really lasted and helped me get through.

On Our Way: The Big $500 Traveler's Check Rip-off

REENI: On the way out, we were reading Abbie Hoffman's *Steal This Book*.[12] All forms of authority were not to be trusted. Rip-offs were outlined. Survival skills were a way to live off the corporate capitalists. We had this outline for lawlessness.

BERTA: I think Mom had given me that book. It gave us the idea for our first big rip-off. We decided to drive from New York to Pennsylvania and, in either Pittsburgh or Philadelphia, pull this rip-off against corporate capitalism.

REENI: We used a few rip-off ideas from that book. There was one we used while getting sodas. They used to have these soda

---

12   Abbie Hoffman, *Steal This Book* (New York: Pirate Editions/Grove Press, 1971). ISBN:1-56858-053-3. A manual on how to survive on the streets like an anarchist. The book was written from a jail by Abbie Hoffman, one of the Chicago Seven but when they were the Chicago Eight.

machines with a glass door and rows of bottled sodas lined up horizontally. Along the rows, the bottle caps stood out and you could uncap them and hold a cup underneath. We made sure we had the can opener and a cup just like the book said—except we didn't use a straw.[13]

The only thing was, we didn't mind ripping off the capitalist bottling company—but we didn't want to deprive the individual person coming behind us of their favorite drink, so we only took soda when there were two rows of that flavor.

Back to the Big Rip-off

Buffy bought $500 worth of traveler's checks—all the money we had with us was pooled. (Buffy's parents may have given her money and I may have gotten money from Mom because that was a lot of money.)

BUFFY: I think we went to Salvation Army or some place like that to buy our outfits.

REENI: Phyllis bought a wig. She got all dressed up in high heels, a skirt, a fancy blouse, and makeup and went to Sears with Buffy's traveler's checks. Phyllis had practiced Buffy's handwriting until it was perfect. She signed Buffy's name to all the traveler's checks and bought everything we needed at Sears: Metric wrench set, another set of tools, and a giant cooler. I mean a big one, maybe four feet, the kind you could sit on. We filled it up with the stuff we needed and bought all the camping gear we thought we would need for the trip. Two hours later, Buffy gets dressed up in a plain midwestern outfit. She even had a tiny gold cross on a chain around her neck. She goes into the American Express office and tells them her traveler's checks have been stolen. They reimbursed her the money.

---

13 Ibid. "DRINKS. When hitching, it's a good idea to carry a bottle opener and a straw. You take the caps off soda bottles while they're still in the machine and drink them dry without ever touching the bottle."

BUFFY: I was scared, so dressing up helped get me into the part. We were very thorough. I immersed myself in the part. We had gone to a bar the night before where I went up to the bartender and reported my wallet was stolen. When I walked into the American Express office, I was nervous: emotional energies came flying out of me, so playing the part was easy.

PHYL: I took a cab to the van after spending the "stolen" traveler's checks. I remember the cab driver. The cab driver and I were both Jewish; in this town that seemed small compared to New York City. We recognized each other as Jews the way minorities and oppressed people do. I was supposed to be "Mary Pat," and he couldn't understand this incongruent piece of information. I had to come up with something to cover our story, so I told him I had been a child of the Holocaust. (It was partially true because my father lost his family in Poland and this affected my conditioning and my consciousness deeply.) I told him my parents put me with a Christian family so that I could survive. He understood this, or least was willing to accept it. I felt terrible that I had lied, but at the same time I told myself, and believed, that what we were doing was encompassing a larger struggle, a confrontation with the system of injustice for all of us, a system that was still going strong around racism and oppressions, and my commitment at that moment was to what we were doing as outlaw radical lesbians. And I was going to meet up with Buffy, Reeni, and Berta as planned! I felt I should look at the bigger picture, as it would benefit him as well, and that he wouldn't be out of the cab fare since the credit card company would pay him. That was really important to me at the time! We had synchronized everything (without cell phones) so that Buffy wouldn't go into the American Express office until I came out of Sears. When Buffy came to the van with the replacement traveler's checks, we drove off to cross the state line.

BERTA: Hooting, in silence this time, our dyke outlaw song.

Outing in Iowa City, Iowa

BERTA: When we got to Iowa City, we met some women at The Hub, a women's center, who were in a women's collective called Ain't I a Woman? Collective or AIAW? Collective. The line was taken from Sojourner Truth's quote made famous during the abolitionist movement.[14]

REENI: There was something really together and organized going on in Iowa City, and we knew it. I think it shaped the rest of our trip. We met the women from the Collective and they said we could crash at their house.

BERTA: We talked politics, we danced, and we swam naked in the quarry. We saw a woman's softball game one night. Seeing all the lights lit up on the field, I thought, *This is what it's like to live your own life*. Great things were happening in Iowa City. Something huge. We could feel it. The fire of possibility was spreading: a lesbian culture was rising up.[15] The spirit of connection became infectious. I came out then. I met a woman named JD in the Collective. We were drawn together by an attraction bigger than anything I had ever felt before. We stayed in her room for two days. I think I drank every drop of her sweat. We talked for hours, and our body parts tangled up like ivy. I kept the wings of that attraction around my heart for years. One afternoon during our stay in Iowa City, I found myself sitting on a grassy lawn writing for hours, filling up a space the AIAW? Collective had said they needed filled for their paper. I wrote a story called "A Gay

---

14 "Ain't I a Woman?" was delivered in 1851 by Sojourner Truth at the Women's Convention in Akron, Ohio.

15 "We Couldn't Get Them Printed," So We Learned to Print: Ain't I a Woman? and the Iowa City Women's Press. Agatha Beins, Julie R. Enszer from Frontiers: A Journal of Women Studies, Volume 34, Number 2, 2013, pp. 186–221 (Article) Published by University of Nebraska Press. For additional information about this article Access provided by University Of Maryland @ College Park (1 Oct 2013 08:20 GMT): http://muse.jhu.edu/journals/fro/summary vo34/34.2.beins.html. 186 frontiers/2013/vol. 34, no. 2.

Fairytale or A Lesbian Plot."[16] The story was about a princess named Snowshoe who lived in a royal family but found her way back to her true home with a group of women in a cave. All men were obliterated in the end. The cave bandits lived happily ever after. Anything being possible.

JD: We were getting ourselves known. There were two day cares—first, they were in church basements, one Catholic and one Methodist. There was such an overflow we made another one—this one in a building given to us by the college (University of Iowa). The building was originally given to a college professor, and he gave it over to the day care because he had kids in the day care. We basically took over these buildings from the college.

BERTA: Looking at JD's bowl haircut reminded me of my mother; The stringbean body was a JD sweet original.

JD: When we were accused of being an elite group from the Ivory Towers of Education, I said, "Fuck you, this is an economic revolution! This is about economics!"

BERTA: Inside, I was chiming, "Right on!"

JD: We were accused of being white, overeducated—a lot of us were overeducated—and upwardly mobile, but I was from the baby boomer generation—the first in my family to graduate college, from a blue-collar family in New Jersey. I wasn't exactly downwardly mobile, but I wasn't exactly upwardly mobile either. We were a particularly forward-thinking group, due in part to the energies of one of us named Pat, who was also from a blue-collar background. She came into the Iowa City Collective as a straight woman with a man who was going to the university. She was a theoretician. There were many strong women in the AIAW? Collective and Iowa City Women's Press: Dale McCormick, Barb Weiser, and Joan Pinkvoss. But we were not about star power—

---

16 From AIAW: Ain't I A Woman? Collective Press, Vol: 2, Issue: 2, (August 27, 1971), 12 pp. Ain't I A Woman?: Sallie Bingham Center for Women's History and Culture, Duke University Reveal Digital Voices.

we worked hard to make power exist on another level. Yeah, stuff was happening then. We were basically making an alternative society. (JD Taylor from the AIAW? Collective)

***

We learned about individual political cells there—each cell serving to fill a need for the community, like day care, publishing, abortion, health care, and yes, a gay cell:

After a long struggle last spring, trying to find a structure to end the frustrating general meetings in which nothing got done, and where we were at different political levels, Women's Liberation in Iowa City finally came up with a structure in which Sisters could be close to one another and grow politically together as well as do things. It was a structure with autonomous cells and a monthly general meeting. Over the summer cells were formed: Publications Day Care, Gay Cell, Speakers Bureau, and the Medical Issue Cell. (AIAW? 1(8), October 30, 1970, 22)

One of the women in the AIAW? Collective recorded their findings, struggles, and political commitment, describing the advent of lesbian-feminist culture, but since one of the agreed-upon decisions of the Collective was to keep individual names out of the paper, there was no signature at the bottom of an article. At one point the Collective signed the name of the Collective itself, "AIAW," as a way to dialogue with readers. The Collective was committed to facing difficult discussions head-on. Lesbian culture was inclusive, horizontal, and open to change. In letters and articles, the AIAW? Collective responded to criticisms and charges of class and race discrimination by noting: first, what was said; second, what was felt—feelings and thoughts examined by looking through the lens of social conditioning—and then, finally, by making a conscious choice to change one's behavior in a way that gave power to all women. The idea was not to blame or judge for our conditioned response but to accept responsibility to change present and future outcomes—each person as a flowering, opening outward with structural support. The Collective which had both—straight and gay—became primarily lesbian in 1971:

Female culture to me means lesbian culture, and until recently it has been invisible and silent... Since gay liberation and women's liberation, since the women's living collective, since new women, women who haven't been hiding all their lives have joined the gay community, Lesbian Culture has come above ground and broadened. (AIAW? 1(16), June 4, 1971, 8)

The paper reached out to include women's issues in other nations, as well as printing information on a basic level to empower women, such as how to fix an electrical outlet. And later came the *Greasy Thumb Automechanics Manual for Women* by Barb Wyatt and Julie Zolot, published by Iowa City Women's Press, Iowa City, IA, 1976. By the time we left in August, 1971, the AIAW? Collective had grown:

We are a collective of 150 women functioning as a worldwide conspiracy of Radical Lesbians. (AIAW? 1(16), June 4, 1971, 22)

REENI: We said goodbye to Iowa City at 2 a.m. when no one was around, leaving our mark on the buildings in town—spray-painting lesbian symbols across them. The spirit of that time was filled with freedom and adventure and possibility. Iowa City helped us shape who we were. And in a way, we were changed after that. When we left Iowa City, we met up with two other women who had also just left there, a lesbian couple. We hooked up with them on the highway. We became a traveling lesbian caravan.

PHYL: Traveling in two lesbian vans was empowering and wonderful. Amazingly we stayed together all across the Rockies. I remember us having to get out to push our VW bus up the hill in some of those high passes. I slept with one of the women from the Collective in Iowa City, too. But didn't disappear for two days! It was one night, and really nice. I remember her mind, her body, the feelings, but not the name! (Turns out it was Pat.) She was very active in the Iowa City movement, and I recall, thinking of her, among other things, as a kind of a theoretician. I wish I could remember the ideas and discussions with more specificity. I remember Dirtbag's name. It left a big impression! Reeni and I spoke on the phone about Iowa City and the wondrousness of finding an oasis of brilliant and strong organized women in the Midwest. Our whole trip changed after that. Very strong experience. And very enduring for me. I had a flashback of the event during the launch of the Obama campaign.

BUFFY: Iowa City. I only remember pieces...the house the women's collective had was big and two stories... One of the women knew of a quarry pond a few miles from where the house was— Reeni, myself, and the woman, maybe others, were with us. We went because it was a stifling hot day in town...it was the first time I remember swimming naked with other women out in the open—that was very empowering.

BERTA: We were swimming away naked and free and getting clean, and some people, maybe a couple, came by and began yelling at us... I think Buffy got mad...

BUFFY: I was always getting angry back then—anger. Mad is not my point of reference, and I was always spray-painting something.

PHYL: I remember an incident of our swimming naked as you say, but I don't think it was at the Iowa City area. I could be totally wrong. We were always looking for places to swim, so it also could have been more than one place. I do know we got into a diatribe with a couple while naked!

BERTA: Some people were standing on the banks yelling at us, telling us that we couldn't be there like that—naked lesbians having a bath.

PHYL: Mostly I remember the enormous lesson I learned through this (as a city girl) of all the land being owned! The concept of private property became super-graphic to me. The fact that the powers-that-be defended "private property," far more than people, and our rights to land and water and life was, and continues to be, a viscerally intense hallmark of capitalism and the work of a police state. And that was some of what we were confronting head-on at the time. This all really struck home to me then, especially as wandering outlaws simply being who we were. The connection to what people who are homeless go through feels closer to my understanding now partly due to our experiences back then.

Butte, Montana: "I'm Gonna Rape Your Clothes"

REENI: When we came to a general store in Butte, Montana, we stopped. It was one of those general stores with a big front porch. There were wide wooden front steps going across where several guys were sitting. I went into the store with somebody. I think it was Berta. I was really into this soda I had discovered. Sarsaparilla. It tasted like wintergreen. And I wasn't given soda growing up. So it was a real find. Anyway, Berta and I went into the store, and Buffy was right alongside of me, but Buffy, being gregarious, stopped to talk to one of the guys. When Berta and I came out of the store, one of the guys had his arm on Buffy's arm. "Don't touch me," she said. The guy was standing on the top step and she was one step below. In one swift move, Buffy reaches up, grabs the guy, and flips him over her shoulder. I knew there was going to be trouble. I ran back to the van and opened the side door and got out the rifle. Back in those days, I only wore bell-bottom, hip-hugger blue jeans. And I always had the top button undone because I didn't like it when it was tight. I was standing there, holding the rifle on these guys, and feeling my pants coming down. So here I am—holding my legs together to keep my pants from falling down, aiming the rifle on the guy. The guy looked at me and said, "Do you really want to point that thing when you don't know how to use it, girlie?" And I said, "Do you really want to risk this girlie not knowing how to use a rifle?"

PHYL: I was over at a public phone calling my lover Jessie. Reeni was shouting toward me, "Get off the phone!" Her tone was urgent, and I remember hanging up abruptly and hightailing it out of there. At first I had no idea what was happening until I saw everyone at the trunk of our bus, and Reeni standing there with a shotgun. And Buffy mad as hell!

BUFFY: I remember pieces of the night that silly drunk man walked and stumbled over to me with whatever stupid come-on a drunk Montana man could come up with... I was surrounded by the power of my sister, and I just didn't care anymore to excuse his stupidity... Part of me was remembering other times I had to, or thought I had to, excuse all the fools who thought they had the right to invade my space and my life... I don't think I was even that good with martial arts... I think it was old rage that woke up. It felt so good to flip that fool and see him on the ground. Especially 'cause in a hundred years, he would never have thought that would happen to him.

BERTA: Looking forward through the windshield while driving away, we talked through a plan. We knew the guy wouldn't take kindly to being one-upped by a woman, let alone a dyke, so we had to figure our next move. We saw the four of them in a car following us. We decided to outwit them by stopping by the side of the road until they passed and wait them out. When the car was passing, one guy was hollering out the window, "I'm gonna rape your clothes! I'm gonna rape your clothes!" I was thinking, *How weird! What is he afraid of? Getting too close to us?*

PHYL: As soon as they passed us, we pulled off alongside the highway and turned off our lights. We waited. And waited. And waited.

BERTA: Waiting filled the van with each of us, one and together. When a song came on the radio that one or another of us could relate to, there would be a stomping boot or a tapping hand. I glanced sideways at the tight curl of Phyllis' head to anchor my buzzing fear. I took in the smell of Reeni's breath over my shoulder: a mixture of tobacco, wintergreen, and Reeni. I caught Buffy's livid eye and was stilled. As if somehow I knew that rage was sacred. I had to stop myself from flashing on earlier times when I had been raped—my fear of annihilation. Surrounded by our outlaw band, rape still fresh in my memory—sure, I was afraid, but much, oh-so-much less so. It was like I now had earth beneath my feet and something strong as fence posts keeping me firm: my sister's boots digging into the ground. Finally, the guys drove off. Like we had figured, drunks don't do waiting well. When they took off, I let out a huge sigh of relief, releasing my fear in our collective breathing.

***

BUFFY: We were on one of our hiking and camping journeys. I think we were in the Dakotas, so I'm thinking it was somewhere in the Black Hills. There was a national park we could hike into with camping gear. We'd hiked in about a day's worth and come to a flat area between trails that went higher into the mountains. In the distance you could see more mountains. We decided to set up camp in the flat wooded area. There was a large clearing. Reeni and I were sleeping in our sleeping bags without the tent. Just before dawn, when the mists of cold can still be seen and you can see your breath, I felt a presence that woke me up. I opened my eyes to a big moose nose a few inches from my face smelling me. That may be one of the first times I was aware magic was there... The moose just stared down at me, sniffing—I just lay real still and watched the moose stare at me. Moments passed and Moose was satisfied, turned and walked off into the morning. Something started waking up in the old part of my Mohawk soul that morning...it was such a private magic moment.

PHYL: Do you remember the time outside of the Grand Tetons where we had backpacked, hiked, camped after we found out George Jackson had died and we spray-painted stores in the town? We were furious and on a rampage. "Free Angela Davis." "Long Live George Jackson." It felt at that time our presence was ubiquitous. Connected to a larger movement. Demanding change. On the way back from the West Coast, we took the southern route and drove quickly and almost nonstop. We wound up making it to the demo at the women's prison in Alderson, West Virginia, which was our goal.

REENI: We decided it was more important for us to be supporting the women in Alderson Prison, so we drove cross-country to the demonstration outside the prison.

BUFFY: About fighting against the prison system: Before we left for our road trip, we went to my hometown: Comstock, New York. Comstock, being the prison town it was—cement-walled, gun-towered maximum security prison, my hometown, nestled in a beautiful valley in farm country in Upstate New York. The prison: bigger than the two rows of guardhouses where I grew up and the two rows of guardhouses down the street where the prison was. The only people who lived in the "town" worked in the prison. In the back of my house, the prisoners worked in a huge farm up a dirt road, as well as in a soap factory down the street near the prison gates. Prisons are all self-sufficient and set up in a feudal system, much like coal mining towns: the warden lives in a mansion on a hill and the "trustee prisoners" are the servants. We went up to my old hometown and spray-painted with all the appropriate slogans of the day—our communiqué to the prisoners who would be brought down to clean it up. We were on fire with a purity of need to make a point to the brothers inside: they were not forgotten. The last word we spray-painted across the warden's driveway: RESIST. After the empowerment of our trip across country ignited our spirits, our decision to drive back in time to show support to the sisters entrapped in the Federal Prison System in Alderson, West Virginia, was a perfect finish to our journey. For myself, having grown up witness to the inequality and injustice—that is, the prison system of this country, it was healing to my soul.

***

The demonstration of our sisters at Alderson Prison was one of the first of its kind. This was a time when women were suddenly regarded as having the same potential for dangerous crime as men. Maximum security and solitary confinement had gone into effect at Alderson, and the sisters inside were striking against the injustice as well as showing support for their brothers in Attica. The Attica Uprising was a frightening example to the world of what prison conditions could bring on. There was a war going on between the oppressor and the oppressed, and that was the way we understood the prison system: As an archaic example of caste system punishment to separate the rich from the poor, the black and Third World people from the insulated white higher classes. George Jackson may never have gone to prison if he were white.

Angela Davis summed it up for us:

The prevailing conditions of race and class invariably result in the captivity of a disproportionate number of Black and Third World people. Our brothers and sisters are usually locked up for crimes they did not commit, or for crimes against property—crimes for which white youths receive prosecutorial, judicial, and penal leniency. George himself was an 18-yr-old man-child when he was sentenced to serve from one to life for a robbery involving $70—one to life—or

eleven years enslavement and sudden death. Through George's life,
and the lives of thousands of other brothers and sisters, the absolute
necessity of extending the struggle of Black and Third World people
into the prison system itself becomes unmistakably clear. (Angela
on George Jackson. Battle Acts 1(8), October–November 1971, 12)

***

BERTA: Those were the days we were changing the world; when
anything was possible.

REENI: I met some women in an apartment in San Francisco
not too long ago. I was visiting a friend there and she had some
friends visiting her from Iowa City, and when I told one woman
my name, she asked, "Are you the famous Buffy and Reeni
who went through Iowa City in 1971?" It turns out that woman
was JD. The last night before we left, at two in the morning,
we went to some public building, maybe even the library, and
spray-painted the sides of the brick in big bold letters: "Smash
Patriarchy! Lesbians Unite!" I was thrilled to be alive in those
times. Those were the best times EVER to come out as a lesbian.
My background had been political anyway, from my parents; they
were big in the radical political movements of their times, and
they were both left-wing activists. So anyway I have background
there, but being in the movement back then as a lesbian was...
exhilarating. I'm really glad I was alive back then.

BUFFY: I remember we were waking up from a lifetime of
choking back and down. I gave birth to a path of personal power
I have continued to unfold... A doorway opened into my deeper
soul...the essence of my spirit. The women I shared with gave
me a solid base to believe in our power as a woman...the need
for us to always stand in the courage of being our power...our
truth. Trusting our heart's guidance and understanding part of
life's dance is to free our higher spirit. When I met everybody
in the seventies, I was still struggling with my own identity: my

Mohawkness was exploding. And that's where some of my rage
and anger was coming from. Revolution was just in the air we
breathed then... Revolution was all over the land for the people
who had been paying attention and instinctively knew things just
had to change.

PHYL: One thing I thought about revolutionary practice came
from being in the women's collective in Windham. The women
who went to Windham to train ourselves in survival skills—to
examine socialist and communist theory from a feminist point
of view, to dance and to trip in nature, to explode into our
power as women, to separate from men and from the oppressive
roles for women in society—were somewhat diverse. We
were about the same age then—twenties and thirties for the
most part—some straight, some lesbian, one woman of color,
others ethnically mixed white of variable class and political
backgrounds. But our force of coming together, at least from
my memory, was the power of women rising, and the power of
the times, of possibility and belief in revolution. The power
of lesbians was on the rise, which pushed some of the women
in the group. But what also stays in my mind is the amazing
camaraderie, sisterhood, and support we provided (and she
for us) for a countrywoman who lived across the road from
the house and land we were occupying. The woman was quite
elderly and was the sole support and caretaker for her seriously
developmentally disabled son. She said he had suffered shell
shock as a child during World War II in Germany, her native
country, which she then left. She understood the horror of what
was going on at that time. Her survival skills were amazing: she
had almost no money, nor independent means of transportation
in that rural area; she worked ceaselessly to raise food, provide
heat with wood, provide medical care for herself and her son
with local plants and herbs, and had some contact with other
locals. In particular, she was in contact with another strong,
almost as old, independent local African American woman who

was equally resourceful, brilliant around use of home remedies, and intensely smart. I remember this latter woman housing and caring for me and my friend/lover at the time when we came back to visit—in a totally direct and un-bullshit way. Anyway, these women, especially the one who lived right across the road from our collective, came into basic and direct acceptance of us and the kind of interdependence we tried to cultivate. She was way ahead of us in some ways, but we learned things from each other and spurred each other on, it seemed, with determination around what it meant to be a woman, with the idea of forging a powerful movement of women, and with a greater incorporation of social wrongs and revolutionary rights. And with the example of what we all could do. And really with love. I got it that no matter where we went, there were women like us, women wanting to be free and as powerful as they were. And not oppressed! That's a lot of what I felt we were doing and pushing for—out loud and angry, wanting to smash the "-isms"—in our lesbian van going out west.

BERTA: For me, being a lesbian feminist included being an outlaw then. Embracing what was alive in us and smashing apart what was keeping us locked down. If we had continued living like we did live back then, I would still be in jail now—or just getting out, prisons now being five times as full as they were in the 1970s and with so many more women. Angela Davis is saying we have over two million in prison today, but back then it was around two hundred thousand. How many lesbian outlaws are being swept under the rug in jail now as if you could erase us? I wonder.

BUFFY: You can't erase me. I'm not erasable.[17] The reason: I've decided to make noise. "Revolution" wasn't a "stage" I passed through. "Living my dreams" was still a fear, guilt, and shame-ridden thought. I took that power back. Now my voice is clear and my spirit demands me to speak my truth. I am no longer ruled by the thought my perspective scares other people—I lived

17 Angela Y. Davis, *Are Prisons Obsolete?* (New York: Seven Stories Press, 2003), 11.

much of my life letting their perspective of who I was as a Two-Spirit Mohawk Woman rule and desecrate me. That no longer happens. Revolution means different things in different junctures in history. Speaking truth from our perspectives and living that truth from our heart is part of being a revolutionary. Not co-opting your spirit to the ruling elite's perspective and way of life is also part of that. Part of my truth is speaking up for my ancestors who were desecrated out of existence—speaking my perspective and truth is part of that. If you decide to include my voice, maybe you can include a disclaimer that my voice has been altered. I enjoy being gay, queer, two-spirit—because I am different and I never wanted to fit in.

Be well, Grow + Thrive, Sister Girl...

RICHTER SCALE

Bonnilee Kaufman

The relatives remarked:
"she's too sensitive,
that's why"
I sense
the fissure,
sense
subtle shifts
middle of the night
rickety tectonic plates
rearrange
I hold fast,
onto the edges of my bed, brave knuckled
from very first tremors
even those minor
less than two point
hardly register on the Richter scale
I sit upright
impeccable
posture on Aladdin's royal blue
gold-tasseled magic carpet,
three wishes
ride out the storm

I sense
the fissure
all my gristle
gathers
like a rope of dust
not strong enough to push
plate glass
doors

reflect eruptions
white pustules on lips
line mucus membranes, render
mouth useless
whoever heard of a tongue
uncomfortable
in its den

Lately too thin
skin cracks
I try to bend down
pick up pieces
but my tailbone shifted
duly left
into back pockets
where money used to be
and I worry
literally spend time
contemplating
near-to
homelessness
and what if I
drop
health insurance
since the landlord
raised rent
and even as I
swallow what's prescribed
shove aside
clumps of hair
shedding
wishes gone awry
I still wait for her
to surprise me,
with periwinkle-blue hydrangeas.

FOR MOLLY/EULOGY FOR A PRISONER OF THE STATE

Cathy Marston, PhD

Molly
was a lesbian
was a survivor of male battering
was the mother of Brandy and Kim

Molly,
with a tattoo on her arm
in honor of her mother's
life and death.
Her brother snubbed her
because of that tattoo,
and told her to remove it.
"I didn't sit in a chair
for hours
to remove it
for YOU,"
she told him.
Quiet Molly said that?
Yes!

Molly had Chihuahuas.
She loved those dogs, too
Talked about them all the time.

On June 19, 2011
I woke up at 1:55 a.m.
I looked out the window—
the ambulance
was on the street.

I looked out my cell door
as I sweltered in the heat
from no A/C
and SCREWED-SHUT WINDOWS.

Molly, EMS brought you downstairs
on a gurney
NAKED
The guards videotaped all the way
to the ambulance

They brought you
right
by
my
door
Then lied
that you were alive.
Your bunkie sobbed and sobbed,
"Oh, Molly! Oh, Molly!"
They took her to seg.

Was it the 105 degree HEAT?
Or was it the Thorazine,
the psych poisons,
I begged you to get off of
that had you so disoriented
that yesterday you wore
your shirt inside-out to dinner?
Was it your bunkie I helped you report?
Was it everything?

To TDCJ, you're nothing
but you're everything to ME,

friend.
43 years old.
You were everything.

P.S. Molly, you'll be
GLAD to know:
law enforcement
showed up 4.5 hours
AFTER
the ambulance left.
Don't take it personally.
I'll take it personally
for you.

DANCING UNDER THE MOON
(WITH OR WITHOUT YOU)

Cathy Marston, PhD

—Lunar Beltane 2011, Full Moon in Scorpio

By day
We move mountains
Forge rivers
Walk across fire
Float on air

By night
We dance under the moon
Light playing
on flesh and curves
Desire culminating
in the ecstasy of Love and Spirit

If you can't hold my hand
and stand by my side
in the light of day

Then
I'll dance under the moon
by myself
without you
Just like I did before you came along

BLACK SATIN DRESS

Nyk Robertson

You stand before me
Continually performing
Appearing to be fearless
Claiming your rebelliousness
Clad in this black satin dress
That flows softly against your breasts
trickling down to your sweet soft toes
As you strike your coached charismatic pose
And recite your practiced polished prose

Of why I should be
the image before me
the picture of womanly best
shoving my being
into this black satin dress
accentuating
my modest breasts
cutting my skin
into the woman
you have learned to be to fit in
tightening the corset
gripping the forceps
you are not the woman
I respect

You are not the woman
you could have been
the woman who defied all men
the one I fell in love with
who has now become my myth

the one who was my muse
who questioned all my views
the one with it all
unafraid to fall
who could stand tall
without a man
holding her hand
without anxiety
about this confining society

You sat in their mold
followed what you were told
took the path of least resistance
threw away your persistence
Now you ask me to do the same
become another name
become another dame
in need of a prince charming
Proper etiquette swarming
Like big bumble bees
Stinging my elbows
To get off the table

I am no longer able
to play your game
of everyone look the same
I have to be a woman
Set free
Become my own being
with saggy breasts
black
dress
less

false less
fear
less
Unable to forget
The women I respect
As I walk these gender lines
No longer deaf and blind

I have seen your breasts
Dress less
I have seen your mind
Rest less
I have held your body
Next to me
Wiped the tears
That got the best of me

Now you stand up in front of me
With eyes of misguided sympathy
You place your black satin dress
Over me
The sleeves slip off my shoulders
My world slowly gets colder
My mind quickly turns older

Your clothes hang on me like a baby asking for forgiveness
As I stand here in this black satin dress

Not man enough to not pay my dues
Not woman enough to fit into you

ADRIENNE RICH:
FRIENDSHIP DOUBLES MY UNIVERSE

Maureen Brady

> Each friend represents a world in us,
> a world possibly not born until they arrive,
> and it is only by this meeting that a new world is born.
> —Anaïs Nin

This woman was small and her hands were knobby, but her gestures were fierce. A bright light emanated from her clear hazel eyes and cast an elucidating beam across territory formerly held sacred as she read from the newly published *Of Woman Born* (1976), then spoke about Woman as Mother not being free to challenge the consuming nature of that role, while Man was free to parent without interference to his career. Herself a mother of three sons, Adrienne Rich's analysis firmly refused to blame the women themselves; instead, she pointed her finger at the system. Low down as I was, on the floor, because I hadn't gotten to this Upper Westside apartment in time for a seat, looking up from her feet to her face, she sent my brain reeling as she dismantled ideas I had long taken for granted.

Deeply stirred, I determined I would be there when next she spoke or read in our city. Never did I imagine we might become friends.

Soon after that reading, I met the woman who became my first long-term lesbian partner and discovered that she, too, was an ardent admirer of Adrienne's work. As an early member of the Gay and Lesbian Caucus of the Modern Language Association (MLA), Judith McDaniel put together the first Lesbian in Literature Panel in 1977, and invited Adrienne to be on it. When Julia P. Stanley, another member of the panel, was coming to New York, Adrienne convened a meeting for them at her apartment. The meeting was followed by dinner, and I was invited to join the party later.

I sat through dinner, trying to look smart and engaged but feeling hopelessly tongue-tied. Judith brought her talent for making a great first impression to the table and talked for both of us. And I was content to ride in her wake. When Adrienne's lover, Michelle Cliff, came in, I liked her immediately. Since she was a struggling, as yet minimally published writer like myself, who frightened me a good deal less, I gravitated toward her. We were closer in age and—with her burnished golden skin, wavy, flowing dark brown hair, large, intense green eyes—she was lovely to look at, as well as witty and smart.

The MLA panel was a rousing success, and we continued to correspond with Adrienne and Michelle. Judith and I bought an old farmhouse that was close to falling down and undertook the devotion of saving it just as Adrienne and Michelle were contemplating a move to the country. When Adrienne asked if we could put her up for an overnight as she traveled from Vermont to Syracuse, we were delighted to go about fixing up a temporary guest room in the midst of our construction project. She stayed both going and coming and, by the end of her visit, expressed that in our prior meetings she had felt I was withholding myself, but now she felt she'd begun to get to know me and liked what she knew.

Withholding! What a concept! I'd wanted nothing more than for her to get to know me, yet I'd created the impression of withholding. I was grateful that she was candid enough to tell me.

Adrienne and Michelle bought a charming old brick house, a former carriage factory, in Montague, Massachusetts. Unlike ours, theirs was in move-in condition. Still, we shared the excitement of setting out the rooms, fixing up our studios and guest rooms, and from the start, we were invited to come occupy their guest room for a weekend.

My first night there, I hardly slept a wink. Two buildings down stood the Congregational Church with its magnificent clock tower, only its bells became great clanging cymbals in my head when they rang every hour and then just once on the half hour, enabling me to count the sleepless hours as I lay awake. *Dong, dong, dong.* Three AM. Sleep, sleep, I admonished myself. Adrienne is going to be so bright and articulate in the morning and you're not going to have half a brain. But then came the half hour, and then the *dong, dong, dong, dong* of the four o'clock hour, and eventually I gave up and just wished for first light so the pain of night would be over.

Over the next several years, I grew familiar with that guest bed and, though the bells continued to ring through the night, I rarely heard them. We shared several Chanukah/Christmases or New Year's celebrations, either in Montague or at our house in West Hebron, as well as other weekends.

In 1979, Judith and I started Spinsters Ink and published my novel *Give Me Your Good Ear*, as well as her pamphlet *Reconstituting the World: The Poetry and Vision of Adrienne Rich*. Once Spinsters Ink became a not-for-profit, we invited Adrienne and Michelle to fill out our board, and we then tried to get together monthly for board meetings. These took place either on shared weekends, or at The White House—a restaurant up on a mountain in Vermont. It wasn't particularly memorable for its food but for the ambiance of its cozy dining room. Seated on its bench seats along the wall, we would occupy a quiet table on a Sunday afternoon for several hours of deep talk and good wine before switching to coffee to prepare for the drive home.

With the inspiration of Adrienne, as well as other women who had become friends, or at least encouraging literary acquaintances—Irena Klepfisz, Joan Larkin, Minnie Bruce Pratt, Carol Seajay, Valerie Miner, Sandy Boucher, Jan Clausen, Elly Bulkin, Frances Hanckel—I became emboldened to believe in myself as a change agent. I went from what had been my hiding place—a sense of invisibility—to the feeling that, just as much as anyone else who was willing to open her mouth or move her pen across the page, I had something of value to say and was going to say it as loudly and clearly as I could. I had been working my way up to this—by joining others to speak out against the war in Vietnam, by helping get Bella Abzug elected. But with this wave of feminism, I moved from follower to leader. Adrienne encouraged me to feel I had something original to say. Even if my words came out falteringly, she wanted to hear them. In fact, there were areas where she felt *I* could teach *her*.

"The personal is political" was our moniker. I had grown up in a working-class farm family, and while not at the bottom of the ladder, my mother had made our clothes from the stiff cotton in which our feedbags got delivered; my sister had developed boils on her head because we only bathed weekly, and despite these sorts of conservation efforts, our farm had gone bankrupt. In spite of my father's earlier rise during the war from the lowly position of wiper (the guy who wipes up excess oil in the engine room) to Chief Engineer, when he returned to the Merchant Marines to man supply ships and oil tankers after we'd left the farm, his salary was meager for a family of six and my mother was forced to work as a nurse until after her children grew up and left home. Adrienne was fascinated by these background details. Her father had been a doctor in Baltimore. Her home had been a fertile place for the intellect, while mine had been a minefield, my father holding forth with contempt for those who worked with their minds rather than their hands.

In those years we were close, Adrienne was deeply engaged with understanding racism in all its permutations, and Michelle, who was Jamaican, as well as other Caribbean and African-American friends of Adrienne, including Audre Lorde, were her constant sounding boards on that. She looked to me for a developing class analysis, which we both felt was lacking in the movement. We had many long conversations about this, and then she would write me a letter the next day or week after we had parted and say, "I felt you were onto something," and her words would set my mind into a spin to try to think further. I offered her my ideas about therapy and class. I felt therapy might steal from the strength of a working-class person who was more survival-based than a middle-class person, because the working-class person's pride was based on getting by, and if her heroism came in the day-to-day achievement of feeding the mouths of those for whom she was responsible, for her, bringing in the interference of psychological trauma might only tear down strength that was needed to go on.

Adrienne and I were also linked by physical pain. In August 1978, on my way to the physical therapy office I was setting up in Glens Falls, a woman spaced out on drugs ran me off the road. My car turned over four times, and not seat-belted, I was knocked unconscious on the first roll and floated about until the car came to rest upside down. Fortunate enough to survive, my scalp flapped open in a huge wound and was literally filled with gravel, for which I underwent surgery. My bruises, contusions, and stretched and strained back muscles would take years to settle down and cease being painful.

Adrienne had rheumatoid arthritis, of which she made as little as possible, but throughout the years I knew her, she graded all of her physical and some of her mental activity against the threat of the pain it caused dominating her, and I was aware of this, starting with each time we'd hug in greeting and she'd surprise me with the firmness of her grasp, despite the involvement of her wrists and hands. Throughout our friendship, as a physical therapist, I dispensed small nuggets of professional advice, and after her first total knee replacement, she came to stay with us for a week so I could work with her daily to rebuild her strength and flexibility. We walked up and down my dirt road, Adrienne inhaling deeply and constructing a haiku as we passed the small orchard where we could smell that special odor that escapes the apple trees when the apples are ripening.

But our main discourse about pain was focussed on ways to keep it at bay, or acknowledgment that we both knew how much of a demon it was as it sat on your shoulder, wanting you to forget about everything else and pay attention to it, when you were hell-bent on keeping your aim on how to break the stronghold of the patriarchy instead. In one of her letters, Adrienne wrote: "I feel I have a lot to explore about the way people in pain are used, objectified, how much energy I've spent hiding my pain because I felt it was a kind of handle on me people could get, in a very superficial way."

When some lesbians began to champion S&M as a means to express one's fantasies, Adrienne and I were flummoxed at the notion that anyone would consider pain pleasurable. Did they not know about pain that one couldn't stop at will or take away? Women like us were derided for having 'vanilla sex' with some contempt, and we took personal offense at that, feeling our pain was being discounted, made into a form of stimulation, rather than the constant drain it was.

The four of us often sat for hours, talking as we shelled peas on the back porch (Judith and I grew copious vegetable gardens as did Michelle and Adrienne), continuing our talk as we cooked a scrumptious meal together and ate it, then moved into the living room, perhaps still serious, perhaps becoming giddy with our consumption of whiskey and wine. If the topic was serious, we might go on late into the night, then get up in the morning and continue to poke and prod at it from various angles. I might string together a couple of insights, but these would dim when Adrienne would get up, hangover and all, to announce a fully fleshed out plan for how feminists should attack the problem we'd been discussing, as if her brilliant brain had continued to work through the night, chasing after loose ends of images we had brought up, and wrapping them up into a cogent strategy.

In those late evening hours, as the drinks stacked up, the conversation might turn to gossip. I was not much of a gossipmonger. I had grown up listening to my mother gossip with others, and it had seemed to make them small. My spinster aunt

Catherine, whom I adored, had also been a big gossip, and while her style of gossiping was more interesting than my mother's, I'd lined up behind my father who held all gossip in contempt. However, now the cast of characters about whom we gossiped were the powerful women of the movement. Women who took themselves seriously as change agents and were working in such earnestness that taking time to gossip about them was almost a way of humanizing and personalizing them. Also, by now, this wave of feminism had grown tight and incestuous enough to generate a backlash of the sort of cannibalizing that seems to go on as movements build in power.

Often the gossip was about who had faltered in her political correctness. Sometimes, we dissected what we perceived as a fault in the work of someone like Mary Daly, who had been criticized as Eurocentric and, thereby, racist in the way she had failed to include Africa in her sights as she'd written *Gyn/Ecology*. We'd reverse the motto—the personal is political—and study the inverse: "the political is personal," and wind up dissecting Mary's personal life insofar as we knew it. I knew her only from a brief meeting, but appreciated her generosity in taking the time to read my first novel and write a blurb for it. I didn't like setting my imagination to work on Mary's personal triumphs or failures, but neither did I want to check the hilarity of my mates as they made up scenarios and screeched with laughter, so I laughed along with them and, I'm ashamed to say, contributed my share of catty comments.

Adrienne was generous with reading my work in progress and gave me great encouragement with *Folly*: "You know," she wrote, "I do feel that FOLLY is potentially a kind of novel that has not been written, that you are drawing into it things that haven't been in fiction before. I really hope that before you go up to Millay (the Millay Colony) you will have real relief from the physical pain and be free to push as far as you can, and want to, on this book."

She sent me early drafts of some of her essays and asked for my response. Often, my comments came down to questioning terms that she took for granted flowed as easily through other people's minds as they did through hers. 'False consciousness' was one I recall pondering. What was false consciousness? Consciousness itself seemed to me to belie falseness. Did she mean pretending to be conscious?

Once, I challenged her about her elitism when it came to poetry, letting her know that I'd felt an implicit put-down of what I might expect to achieve with my fiction when she had said, "Fiction is nothing but a good read." She wrote back apologetically. "Did I really say a few years ago that 'all one wants or expects from fiction is a good read'? I'm trying to figure out what place in my head that was spoken from. I don't think it's just that poetry was, for me, the earliest kind of learning (and writing)—though that is true—but that I had not then ever tried to understand what kinds of fiction really moved and attracted me, and why so many Great Novels left me dead cold... Anyway, I apologize belatedly for that mindless remark."

Always, we encouraged frank and honest critique and thanked each other for coming through without reserve, in spite of the fact that we must have each had a wish for unadulterated praise, at least I did. And I confess that I was carried a bit when she gave me that, as she did when reading *Folly* in draft. "I love this book, and I may have a few bones to pick later, but for now I just want you to finish it." How important it is to a writer to have a reader who sincerely and enthusiastically wants you to finish your book so she can read it! One is still alone in one's studio with the critical voices, but to be able to chime in and counteract them with: "But Adrienne is waiting to see what happens." That went a long way to shutting up the voices made nervous by my taking up the pen. When my critical voices grew loud, I threw Adrienne's weight at them, and thus was able to lay down the next few pages.

Adrienne and Michelle took on *Sinister Wisdom*, the lesbian-feminist journal that had been started by Harriet Ellenberger (then known as Harriet Desmoines) and Catherine Nicholson. Judith and I plunged into our work with Spinsters Ink, publishing several books that would have had a difficult time finding publication otherwise. Adrienne and Michelle took great pains to come out with several excellent editions of *Sinister Wisdom*. We all worked at other jobs to bring in money—whether doing the reading/lecture circuit, teaching, or, in my case, keeping my physical therapy practice going three days a week and writing on the other days. Gradually, we all began to complain of not having enough time for our creative work, stealing from it to fulfill such tasks as packing books, going to the post office, keeping track of paperwork for our respective obligations.

When I was nearly finished with *Folly*, I sent the first half of it to a well-established lesbian literary agent who called me to tell me she was crazy about this book and definitely wanted to represent it. Then, six weeks after I had sent her the complete manuscript, she sent me a confusing letter, saying that while she *should* be taking it on, she wasn't going to. Discouraged by this response from further pursuing the commercial publishing world, I submitted it to Persephone Press, the lesbian feminist press with the strongest distribution network. It was October 1981, and Persephone had grown to the height of its powers, so I was pleased when they accepted it, and that it seemed to have a good running start with lots of people excited about it. Adrienne planned to write a blurb and would later nominate it for the ALA Gay Book Award. I was nervous about the visibility it might bring me, and Judith seemed nervous about this too, dropping statements like: "You're not going to know what happened to you when that book comes out!" Rightly or wrongly, I feared my success might threaten our relationship. In an only partially acknowledged way, our relationship was deeply in trouble already. We were seeing a couple's counselor, a blind woman, who was able to see more than either of us could. My thinking was that we were still very solid, although not very intimate.

That December Barbara Smith and Cherríe Moraga, who were starting up Kitchen Table: Women of Color Press, invited Judith and I, as well as women from a couple of other presses, to meet to offer ideas about how we'd gotten our presses off the ground. When we met in January, at the Staten Island home of Audre Lorde and Frances Clayton, Gloria and Pat of Persephone, though they hadn't yet sent me a contract, greeted me as if I were their new golden girl.

But, by the end of the day, I was down for the count in a verbal knockout by Gloria, who accused me of anti-Semitism when I spoke up for Carol Seajay, a friend from San Francisco who published *Feminist Bookstores News*. Carol had published an article in her newsletter that Gloria declared anti-Semitic. I didn't defend the statement or the article at all. I only said that I found it hard to believe that Carol would have made the gross slur Gloria had accused her of—the "k" word—and I was sure, as a stalwart member of our movement, she would make an effort to right any injuries she had inflicted. My response was an instinctive defense of a friend. I can certainly see now why it was unwise to defend her, but as a middle child in an alcoholic family, I was primed to be a negotiator, especially when anger was flying wild.

Wounded by the vitriolic attack Gloria rained upon my head, I could see no way to move forward with her as my publisher. Michelle, Adrienne's partner, had already published her book with Persephone, and another good friend, Irena Kelpfisz, had her book in the pipeline with them. When I withdrew mine in an oblique way, by requesting they put out a hardcover edition for library and review copies, which they did not want to do, Michelle reacted against me for this and cooled our friendship.

In my heart I knew I had not intended to be anti-Semitic. My education may have been lacking in some of the classic ways that anti-Semitism had been expressed in the past, such as accusing Jews of dominating the media as some sort of a power grab, but given a chance, I was perfectly willing to fill in those gaps. At this time, however, the movement was fully engaged with examining power dynamics and the dynamics of oppression; this resulted at times in an overdone 'political correctness.' For example, the lover of a blind woman told me she was offended at my using blindness or poor sight as a metaphor. And I remember ruining one woman's love of her very beautiful sweatshirt, adorned with an ideogram, by asking her if she didn't think she was appropriating someone else's culture. In retrospect, it is easy to see when we had gone over an edge, but at the time, there was only a righteous feeling of being 'more sensitive than thou' to any possible prejudice or usage that made assumptions about 'the other.'

Although Adrienne was someone we all looked to for political correctness, she did not join in attacking me when news of the December meeting with women from Kitchen Table: Women of Color Press went around the gossip circles. In a letter dated June 21, 1982, she said: "This has been a somewhat harsh period—trying to work my way mentally through what's going on in NY, what's going on in general in relation to anti-Semitism (reports of the Jewish Feminist Conference were mixed), what in fact can be done/written/said to break the paralysis over racism/anti-Semitism, women of color and Jewish women generally... I feel the more I can *know* (facts) on any issue the less likely I am to get bogged down in emotions that are not fruitful." This was typical of Adrienne, the thinker. She thought things through at times when other women tapped into their feelings and interpreted them as if they were *the facts*.

Irena had solidified her contract for her poetry collection with Persephone at the same time I'd withdrawn my novel, and then, just after its publication, Gloria and Pat abandoned the publishing business entirely, leaving Irena's book published but in limbo, while confirming for me that I had made the right choice. This, along with her unequivocal defense of Gloria's attack on me, led to the withdrawal of Irena's friendship with me. My book came out with the Crossing Press Feminist Series, and all manner of odd energy seemed to accost me from various writer friends as I received accolades and good reviews, prominently placed in the feminist and gay press. The lesson I learned from Adrienne then was that the people more successful than you remain free to invite you to keep coming up to their level, while those who perceive they are being left behind want to see you fall.

Judith and I were at odds that winter, and I planned a reading trip for *Folly* that spring without her, unusual, as we had made all other promotion trips together. I drove across country, stopping in five places to read, ending up in Sante Fe. By the time I reached there, having driven several twelve-hour days and sleeping on cots and couches of varying lumps and softness or hardness and exhausting the extent of my extroversion, I was bone-tired and depressed, despite the success of my tour. (I had sold enough books to pay for the trip and been well received at some energized readings.)

Reading Willa Cather's *The Song of the Lark* provided the incentive for me to head to Mesa Verde—the home of the Anasazi Indians up until the twelfth century, when they'd mysteriously left behind an elaborately created canyon civilization. Willa Cather's character had gone there to gather herself and choose a direction for her life—to return to Nebraska and marry, or go forward with her artistic career. And since I, too, was at some sort of crossroads, I hoped a descent to the bottom of a canyon was a way to find some guidance. Driving across country, I had puzzled over what had gone wrong with my relationship. Why had I come to feel suffocated in it? How could we take more space from each other and yet regain intimacy? I had been grieving other losses, as well: The sudden death of my father on June 5, 1981; the loss of Persephone as a publisher in 1982, followed by the loss of my friendships with Michelle and Irena. Indeed, I was awed by what I experienced at Mesa Verde. The harmony of the architecture, the protective descent of the canyon that one had to traverse to reach the ruins, the holiness that seemed to hover around me as I climbed down the ladder into the kiva. I had no words for any of it, but its very air stirred me.

I wanted peace and had been a long time without it.

When I left Mesa Verde, I called Judith and asked her to fly out and drive back with me. I didn't want to need her help, but I did, and it turned out well, at least for the moment. I showed her around Sante Fe and then we camped as we drove back east. Camping brought out elements we liked in each other: quiet moments sitting under the night sky, resourceful cooking, the work of erecting and taking down a campsite together, appreciation of nature, and even the raccoon who came one night to glare at us from the perimeter of our clearing, his stare matching our silent sizing up of each other for our future together, or the lack of it.

Back home, our ties began to unravel. Organizing for the Women's Peace Encampment, scheduled to take place that summer in Seneca Falls, New York, I began a friendship without Judith, with a woman who had an explosive nature just barely contained beneath her surface. This explosive nature attracted me enormously. To sit next to her in a meeting, which I did whenever I got the chance, was to feel as if you were adjacent to the wall of a molten volcano, one working its way to eruption. She was pained by a battle going on inside her, having to do with the way her brothers had abused her, yet my body received her currents only as lust, and lust felt like life to me at that moment.

That spring after my return from the Southwest, I met Adrienne for lunch at one of our halfway spots. Just the two of us. On one earlier occasion, I'd visited her alone in her home and revealed how much my relationship was in distress. She'd said she'd thought it was only Judith railing from being denied tenure, but now (as I was in tears), she could see I needed support and was going to be there for me. I had often solicited and tended to her emotional needs but had not felt her reciprocating much in this way, and had just accepted that this was not her strong suit, but now I thought: Wow, it's just that, with my typical do-it-yourselfness, I've not asked for this sort of support before. But she's saying she's going to be there.

Yet, that next time, when we met for lunch in Vermont, was the last time we met as friends. I was more at peace than when she'd seen me last, and when she asked what I attributed that to, I told her how, although I found it difficult to sit with people who put up aphorisms on the wall like Keep It Simple! Live and Let Live!—how could one describe these as anything other than clichés?—I had made my way into meetings with them and found myself gaining comfort when I lived by their simple slogans. How could this be, I asked her, when I, like her, was about getting to the bottom of things, comprehending the complexity of human nature? This was what I wanted my fiction to be about—finding the depths of a character and, by doing so, showing how that character was connected to others.

"That is the question," she said. "How can you"—I think she stopped short of adding—"believe in this dribble?" I offered that I was living with the paradox because it felt like a lifeline. I know she was trying to listen, but her eyes glazed over and gazed away from mine. She seemed to be sitting on her hands to avoid making judgments, but I felt a wall of ice go up between us. I talked faster and excessively, struggling to reach a point of connection, revealing with more intimacy than I wanted to how wobbly my lifeline had become over the past year, as if I were at risk for falling off the end of the earth. She and Michelle were having troubles of their own, I knew, but I didn't heed how much revealing the threat of our impending split might be upsetting to Adrienne.

There are times when you are aware of a pivotal clashing moment when, much like the huge wave of attraction that drew you together, the undertow begins its pull back into the ocean, magnetic, unstoppable. You go back and forth struggling to recapture your friendship for a month or a year or even years to come, but you always return to that moment when you felt the crack that began the schism. You tell yourself it's so complex, there was this and then there was that, but often there's one moment when one person is mortified by the actions or declarations of the other and the back is turned and then one tends to only be able to see the things that were overlooked before. At least, that is how I perceived my friendship with Adrienne to go down from that moment in the late spring of 1983.

My beginning an affair with the volcanic woman led to Judith's confession that she had already been having one for nine months. I had suspected and asked about the woman who was her lover; she had countered with some stark-faced lies. The lying hurt me the most. Adrienne's term, 'false consciousness,' was this what it meant? Lust was the one feeling that seemed able, even compelled, to arise from the secrecy, and I now knew the source of the energy that had riveted me to that woman's volcanic vibes, driving me straight into her arms, regardless of whether or not I was being true and responsible to my long and mutually satisfying relationship.

Perhaps we still had some psychic linkage because Adrienne called the very night I found out about my partner's transgression. I recorded in my journal: "She was sweet but I think a little drunk. She said she loved me and knew I would come out on the other side. I was glad I told her about my affair. She didn't do any big number on me about it, just said if you're going to be non-monogamous, someone has to start it." Indeed. Little did she know that I had just found out I was not the one to start it! I wanted to set the record straight but, not an hour before, had agreed to keep my partner's affair a secret, supposedly for the sake of the lover who was not 'out.' I would live to regret this agreement, starting in that conversation with Adrienne, who later wrote to say she'd drifted away from our friendship because of my split with Judith, which she perceived me to have been responsible for.

I moved to an apartment in an old farmhouse near Saratoga, taking with me the one cat who had claimed me as her mother from kittenhood, leaving behind our two dogs, who I couldn't bear to separate, and our then charming farmhouse filled with sweat equity.

I may have had a conversation or two with Adrienne the summer of 1983, but our correspondence dropped off, and she began to fade from my life. I grieved through the summer. In fact, I *learned to grieve* that summer. All the angst I had accumulated over my father's death, the loss of the woman I had loved dearly and who had anchored me for eight years, the friendships that had gone south, now spilled over, and I discovered that, more than just passively receiving grief, I needed to participate in it—to stay still, feel my woundedness and heartbreak, and respect the emptiness it created—instead of trying to escape it. It wouldn't kill me. It might bring up a painful past that I had hoped to avoid forever, but to embrace those experiences that had formed the dark side of me was to make myself whole.

In the fall, I started a relationship with a lovely woman I had met at the Peace Encampment, and, of course, I wanted to share my joy with my friends, but some of them, including Adrienne, seemed not as ready for a new relationship as I was. Since then, I have had enough experience with my own shifting feelings after the breakup of friends in couples to know that there are more forces in action than I accounted for. There is the projected threat to one's own relationship: *If this could happen to them, when we thought they were so durable, will it happen to us next?* There is the feeling of offense for the unpartnered partner—that she is being replaced too quickly, that not enough time has passed to give homage to the old union. And there is the sense that parts of the person brought out by the former partner have now receded, and those were the parts you happened to like the best. But when I was the one carrying on effusively about the new partner while hitting a cold wall, I felt only dashed. And wanted to cry out: *If you really ever cared for me, then you'd be happy for me now!*

Adrienne and Michelle moved to Santa Cruz. By 1986, I had started my life all over again. Judith and I had sold the old, restored house in West Hebron, New York, and I had bought a small one near Woodstock, New York, and was living back and forth between there and New York City, where my new lover lived. I wrote Adrienne seeking further resolution for why she'd slipped away from me. I prevailed upon her sense of integrity, telling her I was making new friends, but I could only go so far with trusting them, and that I felt ours had been a close enough friendship to deserve a real ending, a way to grasp what had happened to it.

She wrote back a long letter, bemoaning the loss of that special time we had shared. She ended by revealing that she'd been disturbed by a story I had published, which documented the ending of a relationship. She said she felt I had failed to transform the material and implied that instead of making art of my experience, I'd somehow misused it. Of course, this hurt deeply, coming from one who'd rendered critical judgments of my work many times before, but always with a gentle and encouraging touch. I wrote back swiftly and angrily, hoping to shake the yoke of her criticism off my neck, for as much as her mentoring had helped me believe in myself as a writer, her pithy response now pierced my hard-won confidence.

Looking back from the long view, I see that the movement we had known and loved dissolved just as our friendship passed. Our time of connection was a heady and lively time in which friendships were forged neck and neck with a developing politic, and amidst the creation of a collective literature—feminist, often lesbian feminist—that had not existed before. We started out sharing those books the four of us found in the hidden recesses of antiquarian bookstores and passed on to each other, yet, just a few years later, we could not keep up with the literature that poured from the various women and lesbian presses, and we had each moved into new territory with others whose interests or locales or expectations were more in line with our own.

One of those holiday seasons Judith and I spent with Adrienne and Michelle at our home, Adrienne wrote me a poem on the back of a postcard of a cookhouse in St. Croix, to which was stapled a packet of Carribean spices.

A handful of spice to mix
    with your rice
A packet of hot to toss in your pot,
It's better than soy for conjuring joy.
It's better than holly for Women of Folly
For she who is bold should never
    be cold
Whatever she stirs, the warmth
    will be hers.
When the nights are stern, her
    tongue will burn
So, cheer! Maureen dear,
at the edge of the year

With love from Adrienne

I held onto this poem as if it were a prize all these years, and let it continue to ring in me as Adrienne's message. Regardless of the sting—even of your mentor—be bold, don't let the cold penetrate but stir again for warmth and let that tongue burn. It brings me back to my love of Adrienne, to feeling the delight of a word master and the value of her strong hand flowing across the page, creating her heart-shaped letters which have meant so much to me and others.

The loss of Adrienne's friendship was one of those things I went over and over as years went by, raising and then dismissing the 'what-ifs' and 'if-onlys,' always with a deep sadness. Then, after Adrienne died, and after I had made a visit to a sea rescue hospital in Florida where manatees and other sea creatures are brought to heal, I received the gift of a dream that seemed to release both of us from wherever we were stuck in my psyche.

Sea turtles crowded into a blue, blue pool
Two women, old friends, flopped amongst them
Long gone the sour of estrangement
And even the scrim between the live one
And the one gone over to some other realm
United in dream, they smile and bob
And lift fingers relieved of pain
To wave and promise
Another meeting soon

AFTER MARRIAGE

Tricia Asklar

Say we move the way we did

four years ago, on a walk
that we should have registered
for and realized the danger only later,

waterless and hitchhiking
on the park road. Say our path now
leads us through a forest with blue

fern fronds and also through
barren wrecks of roads half covered
by the eruptions of the past. A stop sign

on no visible asphalt bends over
and directs skyward. You rest
your palms on its red center,

pound it a few times.
Wild orchids shiver at the base.
Say running out of water makes

the hike more vivid, upending
our bottles a practice in penance
rarely taken. We'll find some petroglyphs,

walk carefully too close to danger.
Say we hike along that lava field
with boulder cairns of basalt,

obsidian flashes here and there.
Say we are both still fresh
on the hike and haven't yet run

out of water. You speak in red
tones and the ash clouds drift
off to the sunny side of the island.

Say my name like you did at the start,

let it zephyr into here and now
as we worry over travel
like mutual pariahs.

LOVE THEORY #7

T. Stores

Mari sucked in the sweet fall breeze—cider, leaves, earth—one hand cupping her huge belly, full with twins, watching Christine's car ess down the hill-road. "I am an artist," Mari whispered. "I am not afraid." The construction crew renovating the farmhouse would arrive soon. Not more than an hour alone, she reassured herself. Chris's car vanished behind the last of the golden leaves around the curve. The guys would yell 'Good morning!' through the plywood wall that kept the rain and dust from the three rooms not under construction, and everything would be fine. She would be fine. The babies would be fine. Chris would drive to work and return home fine. Nothing bad would happen.

Mari looked down, over the mound of her stomach. A cricket waddled across the kitchen floor. He pushed forward awkwardly, the little front legs scurrying to compensate for the strides of his oversized back legs. Winter's coming, she thought. Babies coming. "I *am* an artist," she murmured again. "Get to work." She opened the screen door, grabbed the handrail, and trundled the belly of babies down the three steps and across the yard to the studio.

The painting Mari was working on, *Love Theory #7*, would be the last in this series. The show was scheduled to open in New York in February. Her first New York show. Her chance to break out, to be noticed. Her career seemed just about to take off, but the babies were due at Thanksgiving. I might not know much about motherhood, Mari thought, but I don't think I can paint with two newborns around. She sighed and leaned back in her chair, resting her feet on the file cabinet Chris had hauled over in front of the easel. Her ankles looked like the stumps at the edge of their neighbor's orchard, just over the fence beyond the studio. The last painting in this series. Maybe the last art I'll have time to do for months. Mari stared out at the view. The remains of the old trees looked like the short round houses of a fairy village, their younger counterparts stretching limbs to the sky, the last red fruits dangling like jewelry.

The baby on the left side—the girl, Baby A, the doc called her—woke up and jammed a foot or arm up into Mari's lungs. Baby B, the boy, woke up and shoved his butt—or at least that's what Mari thought that was—outward, as if trying to back out through her side. "Calm down you guys," she said, rubbing B's rump through her own skin. She still couldn't believe she was finally pregnant, that the pregnancy had worked, that she was about to give birth to not just one, but two babies. After three years of trying, after all that money spent on artificial insemination, after the miscarriage, they'd almost given up. And now this. Twins.

She picked up a brush and smushed it into the cerulean, twirled it around, and hesitated, marking the vision in her head on the canvas before beginning. A red spot on the edge of the white moved, a ladybug. "Fly away home," Mari said automatically, scooting her away with her pinky. "Your house is on fire...." She bit off the end of the rhyme. The bug whirred away.

Mari rested the hand holding her brush on her knee. How could such a light object seem so heavy? After the first daub, she knew she would lose herself in the painting, into the images, blurring everything else out into parts, colors, lines, textures, juxtapositions of objects, fragments of script—the biochemical theory of love for this one—giant noses, a bouquet in a girl's hand, honeycomb, bees. Until she had to pee again, of course. Or felt nauseous. Or until the fatigue washed over her, as it so often did these days, and she had to nap on the mattress Chris had set up in the corner, the racket from the hammers in the house too loud for sleep. Her hands would swell; she would suddenly feel the pain in her knuckles and focus in on her hand holding the brush, so puffy it looked like a cartoon of itself. Or hunger would gnaw, queasiness threatening if she didn't feed it—feed *them*—again, again, again.

Pregnancy was exhausting. She hadn't realized how much effort it took to grow a human—*two* humans—from scratch. The ladybug thumped into a windowpane and began to crawl down the glass. How had she gotten inside? Why?

Mari heaved a sigh, resisting the urge to sleep. She had to finish this painting this month. She might never have time again. The painting would take her mind off her fears, too. She touched the tip of the brush to the canvas. Like putting the snorkel mask into the Caribbean during vacation last year, becoming suddenly lost in that vibrant and other underwater reef world, everything else—even the babies—vanished.

"Damn," said Jeff, on the other side of the plywood wall. "I forgot the goat cheese."

Back in the kitchen for a late lunch, Mari stood in the open door of the refrigerator, trying to feel desire for something. "Eat as much as you can," the doctor had said. "Eat anything you want." She rubbed the belly. The workmen, too, were on their lunch break, sitting in lawn chairs out in the new addition. Mari liked having them there where she could hear them, close enough so that she wasn't completely alone while Chris was off at work. She was scared to be alone. As October had dwindled with the evening light, she had begun to worry more and more. How much would labor hurt? What if she had to have a C-section? Would the babies be okay? Would Chris still love her body when it was flabby and scarred? Maybe they were too old to be parents. Would the children suffer for having no daddy, for being the kids of lesbians? Bile rose at the smell of something not quite fresh from the vegetable bin, and Mari stepped back and turned her head to breathe the autumn air. Women died in labor. Babies died. And what about my own work, my art? Mari blinked back the sudden pressure of the goddamn tears again. Will I be a good mother?

"Salad again, huh?" Gabe, the contractor, and Jeff and Joe, carpenters and brothers, were funny to listen to. Mari spotted a sandwich Chris must have made for her. They were counting on

Gabe to drive her to the hospital if she went into labor while Chris was at work. Please, god, not too soon, she thought. Another two weeks at least. The babies would be more likely to live if they stayed inside a bit longer.

"Yeah," said Jeff. "I've got to lose ten pounds."

Mari shook her head. How could he need to diet? The guys worked nine or more hours a day, the impending birth of the babies a constant motivator. Muscles rippled in their arms and backs as they swung beams and plywood into place and hefted the nail guns and ladders. A diet seemed impossible. The sixty pounds Mari had gained with the babies—a perfect amount, the doctors said—depressed her. Almost forty, she had still run five miles every other day and done a hundred crunches every night before she had gotten pregnant. Chris had fallen in love with that body, she thought. And now...Mari rubbed her stomach. No abs at all in there. Limiting her food intake again after the twins were born loomed almost worse than did the labor. I'll have to look good for the opening, though, she thought. New York... Mari shook her head. Don't think about it. Eat. She took a turkey sandwich and a glass of milk into the living room and lowered herself into the sofa.

"You don't look like you need to lose weight," Joe said on the other side.

A snort. "You ain't seen me in my Skivvies."

Mari smiled, remembering working in the studio at night a year or so ago, tilting her chin up and keeping her back straight before the easel, imagining the way she looked, spot-lit and visible through the huge windows to everyone who drove down the road or happened to look up from the valley, the artist at work. That woman seemed almost lost, disappearing, swallowed.

"Stop right there," Gabe shouted, laughing. "Too much information!"

Mari chewed, grinning. They seemed to have so much fun together, these guys. Baby B kicked and twisted so that her lower belly rippled under her T-shirt, and Mari rubbed him. She put down her sandwich to lift her hair and drape it over the back of the sofa. That was another thing about being pregnant that nobody told you. Her hair, already thick, had become as lush as jungle vines, a weight that tugged at the back of her head.

"I tried to get him to go to the gym with me," Joe said, "but he's too busy. He'd rather eat rabbit food."

"Heck," Jeff said, "I get plenty of workout at work! I don't get why anybody'd take time off to do more work."

Mari closed her eyes and massaged her scalp, coaxing the impending headache to recede rather than build. She had loved the gym when they had lived in the city. When she and Chris had moved to Vermont, a half-hour away from a good indoor workout, she had missed it terribly. The focus of that hour workout, the routine of it. She and Chris had even met at the gym in Boston all those years ago. Here, she'd become a runner, a skier. An exercise opportunist. Whenever. Whatever. She rubbed the back of her neck. Maybe I should just cut my hair, she thought. It had taken five years to grow out, the whole time they'd been here in the farmhouse. I need a change. Maybe shorter will make me look thinner. Too bad she couldn't go back to that punk look she'd had when they'd been dating in Boston...half-shaved, spiky, wild. That would freak her students out... No. Too old for that now. It wouldn't be me. Whoever that is.

"Baby A," Mari said, washing her brushes out in the kitchen sink at the end of the day, the house quiet with the workmen gone, "you need to stand on your head again. And soon."

That week's ultrasound had showed that Baby A, who was presenting—that is, closer to the cervix and who would therefore be born first—had flipped herself over. Her head was up instead of down. "Swimming in a pool might help," the doctor had said, but the nearest indoor pool was an hour away. The nurse showed Mari some rocking exercises to try to get the baby back into place. "Or maybe you can talk them into it," the nurse said. "Those old wives' tales you know...." Maybe a mother *could* will the fetus to cooperate, Mari thought. As scared as she was of labor, she knew she *really* didn't want to be cut open for a cesarean.

She heard Chris's car in the drive. The doctor had warned that the babies were running out of room. There wouldn't be much hope of turning again in a week or so. To the tune of "Twist and Shout," Mari started to sing. "Come-on, come-on, come-on ba-by, turn it on over; twist and squirm, twist and squirm. Come-on, come-on, come-on ba-by, flip it on over, work it on out...." The babies jiggled with her rocking against the countertop. "You like singing, don't you?" she asked. Baby A kicked.

Chris came in carrying groceries. "Are they listening?" she asked. "Are they moving?"

Mari turned and stuck The Amazing Belly forward so that Chris could see the gymnastics under her t-shirt.

"Whoa!" Chris grinned and put her hand to the belly to feel. "What part do you suppose that is?"

"Elbow maybe," Mari said. She put her own hand over Chris's. She missed the way she and Chris had been before the pregnancy. She missed Chris's body and hers together, parts matching but different. She missed just being together, alone. The way they had been equal partners working together on the farmhouse renovations. Now it seemed so divided, almost like a straight couple, the way she hauled around the belly and Chris did all the housework, the shopping, the yard-work. Mari hated feeling so useless. She hated feeling like a wife, but here it was again. Nobody's fault. "Thanks, babe," she said, squeezing Chris's hand. "Thanks for doing the shopping. For doing everything."

Chris responded as she had done for months now. "Thank *you* for carrying the babies."

Mari groaned inwardly. She was sick of that. *Fuck that,* she thought. But she kept her face blank and her mouth shut. Not Chris's fault.

Mari took the next morning off from *Love Theory #7*, even though she knew she shouldn't, and made an apple pie for the workmen—Jeff and Joe's dad, Eddie, the electrician, and both of the plumbers, Fred and Arnold, had come with the carpenters today. She carried paper plates with steaming slices around the side of the house to the picnic table.

"Oh man," groaned Jeff. "There goes the diet."

"I'll take your piece," Joe offered. "No problem."

Gabe laughed. "You know, we'll keep working even without pie," he said to Mari.

"Just want to keep the workers happy," Mari said, passing out the plates. "And besides, I like to bake. It's apple pie season. I can't help myself."

The guys dug in to their slices with plastic forks. "Oh man," said Jeff. "This is so good."

Mari lowered herself into an Adirondack chair and rested her hands on her stomach, watching them eat, enjoying the warmth of the Indian summer sun.

"Getting a lot of work done?" Gabe asked, nodding toward the studio.

"Not really," she said. "Kind of stuck, actually." She felt a tickle on her bare toe and lifted her leg into the air to see a caterpillar. "Shit," she grunted, trying to lean forward.

"Let me get it," laughed Eddie. He picked the fat brown and black fuzz from her foot and let it crawl across his palm. "Wooly bear," he said. "Whadya think, Arnold? What's she say about the winter?"

Arnold tilted his head back to examine the caterpillar through his bifocals. He'd been their plumber since they'd bought the old farmhouse, thawing pipes for them that first winter. "Well, looks cold," he said, pointing. "Black bands are purty wide." He squinted. "She says the middle'll be the worst. Deep cold in January, February, I'd say."

"Great," Mari said. "Stuck inside with newborns."

"Pipes'll probably freeze too," Arnold said, squinting. He winked at her over his glasses. "This old place keeps *me* plenty warm anyway...."

"You'll be retiring to Florida on these old houses some day," Gabe said, "huh?" They laughed.

Eddie held his hand to the picnic table and the caterpillar trundled onto the wood. "Have a good sleep," he said to it.

"Do they hibernate?" Jeff asked. Mari nodded, thinking of the cocoon she had hatched in a jar when she was a girl, the butterfly emerging, the way its wings had inflated and unfurled before she unscrewed the lid to watch it float away on the breeze.

Eddie nodded too. "That's what I read in the *National Geographic*. They've got something like antifreeze in their blood. You can put them into an ice cube, thaw 'em out later and they'll still be fine, go on about their business in the spring like nothing happened." The business of eating, reproducing, making something of life, Mari thought. Like art maybe. But butterflies don't need their mommies.

"Wonder what they think about while they're frozen," Joe said. The other guys laughed. "Well," he said, blushing under his tan, "you know. Wonder if they have dreams or anything. Brain must keep working somehow even if they're frozen...."

"Caterpillar dreams," Jeff scoffed. "Man...."

"Isn't that what makes the difference between being dead and alive," Joe asked. "Brain working?"

Gabe shrugged. "He's got something there, Jeffy," he said. "We won't turn off your life support if your brain's still going...."

Eddie cut in. "Don't it have to work in the first place...?"

The others laughed again. "Saw that one coming," Gabe said.

Mari shifted in her chair, trying to get comfortable. She grunted, "Uh," without meaning to, and felt the guys become aware of her body again. They were silent for a minute.

"So," Gabe asked, "do you miss work?" He blinked. "I mean, do you miss teaching?"

Mari smiled. He had probably heard her complaining about how people around here thought of her as just a high school teacher and not an artist, about how no one took her seriously as an artist. Those plywood walls.... "I do," she said. "Sometimes." She closed her eyes into the sun, listening to the faraway voices of the apple pickers in the orchard, the screech of a hawk. "I mean," she continued, "I miss the kids. I think about whether they're getting stuff done or just playing around." Mari thought about the AP students for a second and felt guilty. Was the sub helping them put together winning portfolios? And what about slutty, surly Candi in first period? Had she told the sub to watch out for her, watch out for the mood swings that swept in like weather fronts? She was just a kid, just trying to figure out who she was... or who she was going to be. "I worry about them," Mari said. "They're making sets for a drama club production, Shakespeare. Power tools and teenagers, you know."

The guys chuckled. Gabe said, "Oh, I know." He had a teen-aged son, a kid at the bigger high school down in Brattleboro. "They're dumb sometimes, for sure."

"Most of us survive," Jeff said. "Become something. Maybe not much, but something. Most of us figure it out."

Mari knew he was talking to Gabe about his kid. She'd heard him worrying about him to the others, about his lack of ambition, lack of drive, through the plywood wall. "He'd sleep all day if we'd let'im," Gabe had said.

"Yes," she replied. "I think teenagers grow into themselves. What's great about them is that they can imagine it all. They still believe they can make the world perfect. They still think they can have it all."

"You mean we can't?" Joe asked. He stopped his fork halfway to his mouth and widened his eyes. They all laughed.

Mari thought about her days in the studio, all the time she had had to paint this last month without the drudgery of going to school, the time- and energy-suck of having to earn a living. For just this moment, she did have it all. And in a month, she'd have the babies, but what if she lost everything else? Was motherhood worth it? What would happen when her brain—already nearly consumed, like her body, by the babies—switched off, froze up? The caterpillar, a lump of brown and black, moved slowly across the table.

Back inside, Mari cleaned up the kitchen as best she could. She washed out the rolling pin and bowls and wiped down the counter, bending over to reach the faucets beyond her stomach. The apple peels and cores would have to wait for Chris to get out to the compost pile. She really couldn't help herself from baking pies in the fall. Something—maybe the working of the dough, cold with ice water for a flakey crust, or maybe the ritual of trying to peel each apple in one long curl for luck, or maybe just the comforting smell and thick lazy warmth of all that butter and sugar in her blood—calmed her, soothed her mind. She cut another small slice to take back to the studio, where *Love Theory #7* awaited. The hammers rang out again, the men back to work, and Mari smiled, remembering their appreciation of the pie. One of them started whistling. Mari shook herself out of her fog. Back to work, she thought. I must get back to work.

Cramp. "Ohh-uff," she muttered aloud, grabbing her side and leaning hard against the door jam. A contraction tightened the belly. Was it Braxton Hicks? What if she was in labor? She waited, breathing through it, suddenly very tired. It stopped. Maybe just a little nap, she thought. Go to the studio for nap-time, then work. The wooly bear caterpillar can be frozen for the whole winter. In the spring, she's fine, ready to go on about her business of sewing herself into a cocoon, changing into something else. A mind inside ice.

"How do students construct identity in an online classroom where they never meet in person?" Chris asked for the zillionth time. She was on the phone with an old friend, describing her dissertation project.

Mari knew it almost by heart, at least all the catchphrases, and she raised the quilt she was stitching high enough that Chris wouldn't see her yawn. It was only seven. The sun set so early these days, time speeding up as the sun inched south, diminishing as her stomach expanded, a waxing moon.

"Well, they write their identities, of course, in the online classroom. It's the only mode of communication, the only way they can let the others know who they are...." Chris was still excited about her project, and that, at least, made Mari want to care about it, too. She wanted Chris to finish the dissertation, get the doctorate, keep moving. Somebody in this relationship should... She bit her lip, feeling guilty. No. She got to be pregnant. That was important too, something Chris—the doctor had said her eggs were too old—couldn't have. But damn it, Chris was going to have it all—career, family—a full life with no delays.

After the miscarriage, the crush of that disappointment, that sorrow, they had both stalled in their work, the creative work. Jobs had always been the thing they did to make money; writing and painting were the work that mattered. In these last few months during the pregnancy—first, when it seemed clear that it would keep and then with the news that there would be two babies—everything had seemed back on track, the work moving on the tide of their joy, the pace of Chris's dissertation writing, and Mari's painting for the New York opening frenetic with the urgency of the impending births. And the house renovation project—delayed for a whole year—had suddenly moved into action as well, Gabe nailing up the plywood walls that would divide them off from the upstairs (fine, since the doctor had forbade her from climbing them), the machines arriving to knock down the old enclosed porch with the tilting floors, to excavate stones and earth and the perennial garden for the new foundation, the concrete poured, the framing and roofing, the school-year begun, and then her maternity leave. Reduced activity. Everything would change again when the babies came. But how? Mari thought of the Love/Theory series. Why couldn't she finish this last piece? She had to get it done.

Chris had started a fire in the woodstove. It heated their three rooms quickly despite the draft around the edges of the temporary plywood walls. The windows had been delivered today, and the men would install them tomorrow, enclosing the addition a little more. Then the insulation would go in, then the drywall and trim, then the floors. Arnold had roughed in the new upstairs bathroom, and Gabe said he'd get the stair landing done while Joe mudded the drywall. Mari couldn't wait to be able to see the work upstairs, the new dormer that ran the length of the two bedrooms and new bathroom. She wanted to be back in her own bedroom, newly light and airy, open to the view of fall colors on the hills, and she wanted to get to work on the babies' room, choosing the colors of the walls and arranging the cribs. But that was probably just a dream, Mari thought. It would be at least another month of work before Gabe finished. They would all live downstairs until the guys finished the work, the babies in the same crib, all four of the family in the three rooms with plywood dividers.

"So I'm tracking the references students make to themselves in the online discussions," Chris said into the phone. "Especially in ways that seem to help others see who they are in the real world outside the class." Mari thought again about her painting. How was that annunciation, those bees and hives, a communication about her? What was she telling the world?

Mari pulled the needle around the edges of the beaver shape on the baby quilt. Each square had a different animal shape. Mari had made so many of these quilts for other people, for friends, but this one would be for her own baby. For one of her babies.

"Right," said Chris. "Like they're building who they are for others to imagine."

The animals on this quilt were all from New England, animals the babies might see: a deer, a red-tailed hawk, a moose, a bear, a cricket. Mari hadn't decided what to put on the other quilt, maybe exotic animals, like lions and monkeys, or domestic animals like cows and horses and pigs. Maybe something completely different, like toy shapes or food shapes. Maybe city shapes. Would the baby with a New England animal quilt stay close to home? Would a baby covered by city shapes or exotic animals grow up to move away? Would a baby warmed under the images of farm animals become a farmer? Mari smiled. She wondered what identity she was sewing for herself.

The painting *still* wasn't right. Mari had been staring at it for an hour, her hands resting on her stomach. The sounds of hammers from the farmhouse were muffled, the guys working inside. Chris was off at the university again. Another week of waiting gone. Another last minute of painting vanished forever. I have to finish this, she thought, rubbing her stomach; the clock is ticking. What is it about this one, #7?

The painting was complex, incorporating a medieval annunciation scene, but changing the dove that is supposed to be God impregnating the Virgin into a bee stinging her, and outlined with text from Dante: "In the middle of life's journey, I found myself in a tangled forest that obscured from me the wanted way." Something was still missing. Mari always worked intuitively on a series, usually beginning with theme—love, in this case—which she researched in the library, finding for herself the ways the idea had been theorized over the ages, discovering the images from art history and contemporary culture that expressed her own, usually feminist perspective on that theory. Sometimes she tried to make fun of the theory, like with #3, on Freud, into which she had painted a hot dog and donuts. Number 7 just wasn't yet right. She tapped the paintbrush on the glass pallet. What was missing?

"Fuck it." Mari let her paintbrush drop to the table. She looked around the studio. Crumpled paper towels blotched with paint littered the floor. Old computer printouts, ashes from the woodstove, Styrofoam peanuts from an unpacked box of canvases, and empty plastic water bottles added to the clutter. She had to clean. The house was a disaster of sawdust and muddy boot tracks, and she couldn't do anything about that until the renovation project was finished, but at least she could tidy up the studio. Mari grabbed a broom and started to sweep, jabbing at the windowsills and edges of the baseboards. The babies were quiet inside, rocked by the rhythm. On the south wall, she tilted back a stack of blank canvases to sweep behind them. She gasped. Hundreds of ladybugs lay like little drops of blood on the grey painted floor. What the heck? Mari hesitated. What could she do? What had happened? She gave herself a shake and swept the dry husks of the bugs into the pile of dust and trash.

She rested, leaning on the broom, and looked out. Through the window, the sky was a brilliant fall blue, the leaves just past peak color. Now that it was cool, Chris started a fire in the woodstove for her in the mornings on the way to work. Mari paused, looking down into the orchard next door. Beyond the stumps, apple pickers, the Jamaicans who came each year to work for Zeke and a smattering of white kids in their twenties sporting beards and dreds, perched on ladders, bulging sacks over their shoulders, the red fruit like ornaments in the trees. The orchard was organic, and Zeke had good luck recruiting pickers from the co-op bulletin board and the vegetarian restaurant to supplement the black men who had been coming from the islands every year for decades. She herself had picked apples when they moved here after she finished grad school, looking for a place to make a home, a community where being a lesbian couple was no big deal, and where they could actually buy a house and a little land with the money Chris's grandmother had left her. They'd both done whatever work they could that year— substitute teaching, farm labor, house cleaning—to make ends meet while painting and repairing the old house and converting the barn into a studio. And then Chris had started work on her doctorate, and Mari had landed the high school teaching job, and they'd started trying to have a baby. Picking had been hard work, dawn 'til dusk. Mari stretched her back; the ache from carrying the twins was not that different from that she'd felt during apple picking...but at least then, she'd been able to sleep comfortably at night. The Jamaican men did most of the tree work, their thighs and backs and arms muscled hard, and she and the others had packed the big crates and hauled ladders. It wasn't the physical exhaustion that had made her quit though. It had been the yellow jackets.

They were everywhere, drawn by the sweet stickiness of bruised and bleeding fruit. And she hadn't bothered about them at first, had ignored them like everyone else. Then, her third sting in one day put her in the hospital, unable to breathe, her heart pounding, the adrenalin making her feel so much rage that she had punched the nurse who was trying to give her a sedative. "It's typical," the woman had told her later. Luckily, the nurse had ducked, avoiding most of the blow, and Chris had stepped in to hold Mari down. "The fight or flight response. Bee sting reactions trigger it, make your brain go a little haywire. Don't worry about it." Remembering, Mari felt her embarrassment all over again. She hated losing control of her emotions, her body, like that. Of course, she could have died.

One of the babies stretched, pushing into her bladder. Mari gasped with the sudden pain. "Ow!" she said. Damn. She had to get to the bathroom again.

Gabe looked up from his table saw as she rounded the side of the barn. "Hey," he called. "You okay?"

Mari nodded, grimacing. "Sure." She felt like throwing up.

Gabe frowned and started over to her. "You don't look okay," he said.

"Just gotta pee," she said. She gripped the railing of the steps to the kitchen and took three deep breaths. Her belly constricted. Contraction. How many others had she had today? Should she start timing them?

Gabe's small rough hand gripped her arm under the elbow. "Let me give you a hand," he said. "Take it easy."

"It's going to hurt, isn't it?" Mari heard herself say. "The labor." Gabe helped her into the kitchen. "You were there when your boy was born, right?" She heard the note of fear in her voice, but she couldn't help it. What if something went wrong? Things did go wrong at labor, especially with multiples. Mari swallowed, trying to hold down the lump in her throat. She wanted these babies to live.

Gabe shrugged. "Yeah," he said. "But it wasn't me giving birth, you know."

Mari stopped at the door to the bathroom. "I'm not going to die, am I?" she asked.

Gabe held her gaze, not smiling or laughing, and shook his head slowly. "No," he said. "You're not going to die."

"I was an idiot," she said to Chris later, back in the studio. "He must have thought I was nuts." Her neck and cheeks burned. "Damn! Damn! Damn! Damn! Damn!"

Chris massaged Mari's feet, propped in her lap. "I'm sure he understood," she said, her voice low. The guys were working late at the house, and Mari had awakened from her nap to the smells of drying leaves and frost and sounds of hammers and Chris opening the door. She had almost cried with relief. "I'm sure he doesn't think anything except that you're a pregnant lady with lots of chemicals floating around in your blood. Hormones."

"That's a crappy excuse," Mari moaned. "I hate people thinking I'm crazy. Oh shit, I am so tired of this." She laid back into the pillows. The babies fluttered in her abdomen.

"Gabe doesn't think you're crazy," Chris said. She squeezed her foot. "You're not crazy." Her voice was low and steady. "Things can go wrong, but nothing will. You'll have the babies, and the guys will finish the house, and winter will come, and we'll tuck in together, safe and warm while it snows."

"And I'll never finish my paintings," Mari said. "I just can't get this last one." She nodded toward the easel. "And the show is coming up and I'll never have time to do it after they get here." She swallowed and bit her lip. "I'll never be an artist again."

Chris took her hand. "Of course you will," she said. "It's who you are."

"Really?" Mari said. "Is it really who I am? It is now, but will it be next month? This winter? Next year?" She felt A flipping around, wriggling into B. She patted her belly, the babies. "What about them?" she asked. "Will they let me be an artist too?"

Chris pushed Mari's feet off her lap and stood up. "Yes," she said. "They know that's who their mommy is." She walked over to the window and stood beside the easel, looking at the painting. "It's great," Chris said. "I love it."

Mari watched her lover's eyes—squinting, moving around the canvas, back and forth, pausing on something, moving to consider something else, going back, reading across the text, blinking. This was the woman she loved. This was the family they had made. Chris wouldn't let her get lost. She'll keep reminding me. The work, the ideas, the joy. All of it.

"Do you think you can't finish it...," Chris began. Her eyes met Mari's. "Do you think you can't finish it because you need to start the next work first? You know, like I have to know what I'm going to write next before I can let go of something...."

Mari blinked. They had had this conversation before, over and over again throughout the ten years of their relationship. The new project had to be conceived before the old project could be completed. Why hadn't she thought of it? Mari pushed herself to her feet and walked over to stand by Chris. She leaned against her. "Maybe," she said. The dark windows seemed to frame the two of them, standing close like this in the light, The Amazing Belly protruding toward the easel. Mari thought of what they would look like to the person driving by, or to someone looking up from the valley floor. "But I can't even imagine what will be next," she said. "I don't know who I am going to be."

Chris hugged her close then, tight to her shoulder. "Oh, babe," she said.

Something on the floor moved. Mari blinked. The tidy pile of dead ladybugs, the ones she had swept together from the south wall, were scattered again, individual red dots spread out across the gray board floor. She leaned around Chris to see better. One moved, crawling away from the heap; then another fluttered a wing; and another one took a tiny step. "They're still alive," she said. "Look." She pulled away and pointed.

"Wow!" Chris said. "Where'd all those ladybugs come from?"

Mari bent a little, hand on the windowsill. "I swept them up when I was cleaning earlier," she said. "They were all over the place." She watched as another one labored away from the pile of bodies, headed toward the wall. "I thought they were dead," she said.

Chris laughed. "I heard Eddie telling Gabe that the ladybugs were coming in," she said. "I didn't know what he was talking about." She knelt down beside Mari for a closer look. "They hibernate inside the walls and under the baseboards if they can find a way in," she said. Chris put her fingertip down to touch one. It climbed on. Chris held it out to Mari, the smooth round shell glinting like a ruby, the little stick legs walking deliberately across the hairs on the back of her hand. "Not dead at all," she said. "Just taking a little nap."

When they walked into the kitchen, it took Mari a minute to register the change. The doorway had been opened. Over the counter was space instead of a plywood panel. She could see into the new room. "Wow!" They both stood still for a minute, staring. The black of the windows reflected Gabe and Jeff and Joe, who had stopped working when they entered, grinning back at them. The space was enormous, bigger even than she had imagined it. Chris squeezed her hand. The studs were still exposed and there was no railing at the stair, but it was a room, enclosed, a part of the house, a bigger house.

Mari felt the babies flutter low down in her womb.

Love Theory #7 could wait. She could finish it in winter, even encased in ice and snow. She would find the time. Chris would help her find the time. She'd find something new, she thought, fingers laced over her belly. Some new subject to paint, some new idea, new passion.

Gabe moved suddenly, stooping low. "Got'im," he said. He held his cupped hands to the window and opened them. The cricket inside hesitated, then sprang away, backward into the room instead of out into the night.

Mari laughed, her voice loud. The cricket scrambled under the stair despite the carpenters' chase, Joe finally sliding on his knees, Jeff lying on his back on the subfloor, laughing. Gabe shrugged at her, palms up. Chris squeezed her hand. "How about a beer, guys?" she asked.

"I been thinking about that pie all day," Arnold said.

Mari felt the babies flutter inside, an insect feeling. She thought of *Love Theory #7*. She thought of her next life. The cricket chirruped, loud in the big new room.

THE WRECK AND THE BUTTERFLY GIRL

Kat McAllister Black

i. Isla Perro

There was not much left after pledging
myself to my first love in a Spanish cathedral
but to fuck her ex-girlfriend in too many bathrooms,
dispersing the clamorous moons of her breasts
like the awnings of jellyfish
I palmed away in Guna Yala. Her fiance's snaggle-tooth
combed through my flesh like fire coral as I
downed shots to mute my body's permutations:
impaled on a toilet, wedged against a bathtub,
drowning on the tile or shimmering like a wreck
thumbed by lionfish, portholes clenched against their spines.

ii. The Butterfly Conservatory

In an opium den of winged junkies
Blitzed on tropical fruit, we sipped
at each other's histories, *Were you inpatient or outpatient*
and *My first was a Dutch pilot,* as
their legs, long as ring fingers, forced open
their umbrella-drink bodies between our thighs,
separating us like piano keys.
Each cilia-soft beat on my own
bare calf struck oil in my skin, threaded new nectars
through me like aneurysm coils until my cells
rattled their panes. We flitted around
the rims of martinis and kissed for hours under
the 100-watt porch lights of male eyes in bars, until
punch-drunk on your perfume and the lace

trimmed close to your curves by sweat, the way you pulled
at your beaded arms like taffy, I homed in on your rib cage
limp-winged with want, and I drank, drank, drank.

Just one last hit of you in the streets of Northampton
    is all I ask.

ECHOES

Ronna Magy

For years I've slept with the television on, trying to forget the sound of her voice, the memory of her skin, her dark hair and round face, soft, brown eyes, her words in my ear. "Hon," she says, and with her stories takes me back to life growing up in Russia, a wide-eyed child in the midst of a cold, poor nation, a Jew amongst anti-Semites, post-revolution, red scarf tied around her neck.

Because of her, I no longer romanticize Lenin and Stalin, the Russia of 1917, or the Chinese Revolution, the way we did in our twenties, carrying around the Little Red Book quoting phrases from the Great Chairman Mao with his visionary dreams. Because of her, I can see what revolution looks like after the overthrow of the bourgeoisie while the red flags are still flying, after the party members turn to bureaucrats and the everyday people have to barter for heat in winter, extra pieces of fabric for clothes, and for chicken to make soup.

Because of her, I know more about the erotic zones of the body and the sensitivities of the flesh. What love feels like when from under sensations it cries out to be heard. Perhaps I didn't truly know love until I met her. Her long dark hair and the fullness of her lips. The way her tongue caressed my mouth as though I were a divine morsel. The arousal of every part of the body, every space, and those I didn't know before her touch. The way my skin breathed beyond its pores after she'd been there.

Because of her, days near the ocean with waves lapping on the shore were enough. Days walking the boardwalk and the sand underfoot were enough. Days spent lounging in striped blue beach chairs in the warmth of the sun, the ocean breeze, and the lull of summer were enough to make us lost in each other's flesh, moans and cries, and dreams, and all that too, was enough. Filling us and the days till we needed no more.

I am changed because of her. Because of knowing her thoughts and questions of "why" asked of things that came so naturally to me, they were like tongue and lips and skin and shadows that were there and not there and there again. Changed because in knowing her I became open to new ways of life and love the way one is when she enters the realms of the unknown. And stays until there is no more.

VORTEX

Dinah Dietrich

I'm so mad my hair could burst into flame

I look back
down the dark vortex that was life
that consumed me, swept me in
the blackness, a nightmare

that dark vortex
kept me for years
swirling

Now I close my eyes
see whirling blue sky
dizzy swirling blue

Now, healing
broken open like a geode
the starburst of joy
shimmers often

JEREDITH

Diane Furtney

Teasing, I said
to the back of her head:

"Why any two people take up together
and define each other

as a need, is not as hard to understand,
considering the hand-in-hand,

paper-doll nature of first desire,
as why it is that certain lovers do not tire."

She rolled to face me, bent her arm
to prop her head, and smiled: the sum

of oddity, she who was happy
in a marriage and could marry happily

again. How is it she can recognize
so much, including evil in its tiny, pale disguises,

but the knowledge does not alter
her kindness? She has sophistication without the falter,

without the embitterment that hits like a wind,
sharp and reasonable, when you turn a corner. Send

for that everywhere, look high and low.
Minute to minute how she exists, I don't know

and I would like to know. She's apples
and oranges? She's an inclined plane that rattles

as it rolls a ball to spring
a switch that rings a bell that swings

to light a flame? That's how she works? No,
probably not: the Rube Goldberg gizmos

of the heart sooner or later
over-heap and totter

and by now would have collapsed.
"Are you partitioned?" I've asked her. "Apsed?

Do you experience A through L, for instance,
in some spacious section of your mind, then advance

to another, larger room?"
What is she up to? We are as doomed

as any others, of course. Time has not
altered its nature on our account.

It uses her and me as it uses you, to express,
not always interestingly, its fields of stresses,

including days attenuated or over-dense.
But who wouldn't stay with her? She makes no sense.

SAILING TO MYTILENE

Diane Furtney

To a young woman at a bus stop in San Francisco
and for anyone young and lonely

It's not as if I don't remember
that concentration, the fever

of waiting, alert for a sign
that the world (with all its confines

of structures and premises, any of which,
it seems, could be changed or switched),

that the world actually
might have moments of less difficulty,

less unease. There's a tautness
in you, a fine almost-overwroughtness,

listening to everything...
Your eyelashes are another small, stringed

instrument. You are a bright conclusion,
what the world in any of its persuasions

calls beautiful. And the waves
of traffic past this broken-paved,

crowded, bus-stop corner
are racketing with a purpose to more

than—what, a thousand destinations
per hour?—Mytilene, only one

among them. We stand apart.
I won't see you again, we aren't

likely to speak. And maybe
because your hopes are so solitary,

so much at risk for self-despair,
I have a wish for you. I'm sure

no one's pronounced it, ever,
on your behalf, and it's one I'd offer

as unpresumingly as possible, just for
your inner ear. It's a wish for

luck, of course, but only of a certain
kind, not the poses and protestations

you're all too likely to find
the sea of the real world delivering, end-over-end

into your life. Those wastes: the pouts
and sullenness of "love" that then turns out

to lack empathy and deep world-interest
while keeping a fierce agenda about its past;

also the drunk or clenched or over-layered,
the sexual wanderers

and the sexual frantics. Or the blur,
awful, after small but elongated failures

of sincerity, when feelings have been
explained too little or too much. Or the line,

fraying, with which you'd anchored
—feeling incandescent, delivered—

in someone who then becomes
half-hearted, unconvinced. Or some

other—Well, but what do you really
want, I wonder?, vagrantly

young, whom I imagine I know about.
You look inward, then out

and down the street, you both notice me
and don't, a fact my vanity

registers as good and bad.
And as one who'd be glad

of a brace against vanity's maraudings,
what I wish for you is something

altogether else: the lover who is not
your heart's desire, not

your type, you think, who instead
is almost uninterestingly good

for you—something like, say, piscine
vegetables. Someone, I mean,

with whom the imagination,
always a slave at the oars, awash again

with self-dislike and rancors,
can find enough scope for

the daily, large and tiny
efforts at restraint and loyalty.

I know if you're extra-fortunate,
that lover's traits will duplicate

those of my own love—who's clumsy at
times, aggravating, not

invariably endearing, a strange thing,
and whose gestures are like something

that skims and elegantly bends
above the long depths of her mind.

Once, in closeness,
she asked aloud—she is that generous—

"How much would I give to be
here?," and has described my body

as "those serious and glamorous depths."
Braver than I, deft,

she's another knowledgeable reptile,
able to interfere with certain of my perils,

with one or two of my undoings.
So my wish is not for vanity's dreaming

imagery, a best-that-turns-into-the-worst,
but the awkward, reversed,

and harder dream, the one so desperately
at odds with your fantasies;

may it arrive, as it usually does,
like a simple packet boat you somehow recognize.

Possibly lost, desirable: that I won't know
what becomes of you, that you won't know

that we have met—well,
there's a decorousness to that, I suppose, a still

surface I would not disturb,
just ripple lightly on this momentary curb

with a story, something permanent you make me
think of, from Thucydides.

The Athenians, fifth century BC,
exultant after a long-embattled victory

over one of their most stubborn
and unruly colonies in the Aegean,

sent off a full-geared warship—late
in the day this was, after detailed debate—

back to the defeated island
to carry out their sentence and command:

that every citizen of its capital,
Mytilene, be put to death. But full

of misgivings through the night,
next morning they reopened their debate,

argued until afternoon, re-voted, and dispatched
a second ship to try to catch

the first before it put to shore,
to rescind their execution order.

Under this sky like the blue of waves,
for you as well, may you have

swift winds: the trireme
of self-hatred, sleek and trimmed

and low in the gorgeous water,
may it be overtaken by the faster

ship of mercy. Or, leaping from the anchor
like the Greeks, race from the harbor

to the assembly in the square
—where swords already glint, lifted in the air—

in time to save the old, decayed,
impoverished, noble city. And may

you find, still breathing
under the conquered walls, something worth saving.

Note: See Book III, Sections 3.35–49, "The Peloponnesian War," in
The Landmark Thucydides, Robert B. Strassler, ed. (New York: The
Free Press, 1996).

MUTAGENIC DIASPORA

Michelle Lynne Kosilek

Imagine being homeless and simultaneously immured within your body. This bizarre incongruity is the context in which transwomen experience our Diaspora, imprisoned in exile from the homeland of our female selves. When our very essence is refuted by external mechanisms—along with our dignity and humanity— our internal struggles are magnified by these misinformed lenses of political and/or religious opposition. The voices of our true selves fill our little girls' hearts with screams of protest, confusion, and anguish. I've been screaming inside since childhood, when a nun locked me in a closet over night for daring to wear a dress. Since then, I've learned that exile can be multi-dimensional.

One of those dimensions is our inability to conceive. While natal females have mostly been freed from the patriarchal slavery where a woman's value was inextricably linked to her willingness to be subservient and to bear children, some transwomen are still in their thrall; our continually breaking hearts playing the role of ironic, intransigent slave-mistress, insisting that only a functional uterus can set us free. Despite advances in corrective surgery, this option remains as elusive as lasting peace in the Middle East, and most insurance companies still don't cover the cost of gender-affirming surgeries, to say nothing of uterine transplants.

For prisoners, even more obstacles exist. Most prisons provide no treatment for Gender Identity Disorder (GID), and the few that do allow only counseling and in some instances, female hormones. Most also deny access to female clothing and underthings—even if we have breasts—and makeup. Attempts to use readily available items like grease pencils or highlighters result in disciplinary reports. In Oregon, transprisoners are punished for shaving their legs. In Kentucky, all prisoners placed in Disciplinary Segregation for even minor infractions have their heads shaved!

This is the context in which I dared to seek gender- affirming surgery, the Holy Grail of GID treatment. On September 4, 2012, I finally succeeded, raising the hopes of six hundred plus other women like me currently in men's prisons in the United States. After a twenty-year legal battle, Judge Mark L. Wolf ordered the Massachusetts Department of Correction (DOC) to provide me with the gender-affirming surgery their own doctors had recommended years earlier. His 128-page decision confirmed and validated every claim I'd made in my memoir, *Grace's Daughter*, about two decades of shameless malfeasance by a succession of DOC commissioners. One of the DOC's trial experts tried to bolster his disingenuous testimony with some particularly abhorrent male elitism, that disease that prevents some from knowing that all women are beautiful. Chester Schmidt told Judge Wolf that I shouldn't be allowed to finish my transition surgically because my female presentation wasn't flawless! Had he known that I'm a lesbian, would he also have questioned my lifetime commitment to my lovely Jessica, my light, my muse, my silky-soft treasure trove?

As I await the DOC's decision to appeal this precedent-setting ruling, my thoughts keep returning to my six hundred plus sisters. How many years will it take for one of them to be blessed with the rare triadic complement of a compassionate prison doctor, diligent lawyer, and courageous judge? Depending on whose statistics you recognize, this isolated sorority has a subset of sixty to 120 transwomen who are also lesbians. Condemned to wander in the desert of misogyny without the companionship of other women, they are as isolated as any women have ever been. Most will be denied any treatment for GID, while surrounded by men who will try to rape them with hate-speech and sexual assault. When their lives become intolerable, the most likely DOC response will be to isolate them in the same segregation units where the prison's most dangerous prisoners are held. These obstacles to their homecoming will remain as intractable as Donner's Pass was, and their starving hearts will feed on an equally-desperate menu, from self-castration to suicide.

Until we force prison reforms with our insistent, relentless, all-embracing feminism, our sisters in men's prisons will never be freed from their onerous exile. It's no secret that the T in LGBTQ is still experienced as an embarrassing relative in isolated pockets of our family. This chasm may not be as wide or deep as it once was, but if it's large enough to keep families estranged, it must be filled with our love. We have so much, and their emotional harvest is scant, and mostly bitter.

I've been more fortunate than most, including almost complete acceptance by female medical and mental health staff. Their correctional counterparts have been less gracious, a resistance that seems to increase proportionately as their rank increases. I can hope at this point that when I'm transferred to the women's prison, the universality of women's sorrows and joys will demand more of them. If I can't end my exile in the one place where I should finally feel free, then I'll have to keep screaming.

My dream of being a country girl, shuttling between my poetry and garden have been deferred, but if my silence keeps me in exile how will I ever help my sisters to find their way home? If we don't claim the authorship of this narrative of emancipation, the hateful words of our detractors will continue to stake a claim in the spaces that our collective joy should have immunized. We cannot, we must not allow hate and ignorance to eclipse our beautiful dreams with the shadows of their fears. As women, as lesbians, as feminists, we are stronger and more deserving than that.

ENJERA

Red Washburn

I.

She met her on 14th and U, just off the metro across from Ben's Chili Bowl, with all its grease and all its riots, not far from the most unimportant house in the country. She was late, a genetic defect, distracted by the stillness of words. She met her atop the escalator, towering over her with smoke lassoing them before arms welcomed smiles, curved like cantaloupe wedges. They shared Almaz Ethiopian Restaurant's vegan combo for two, loaded with lentils, string beans, potatoes, and cauliflowers. No fishy business. They fumbled for food, grazing the soft life between each other's fingers. She imagined sucking her fingers one at a time, as if they were the right sulci of her brain. Their eyes protested blinks; their minds syncing metaphors. She went to the only bathroom with two toilets in a one stall. She felt her eyes undress her before she released the toxic she was holding in. Her knees welcomed her back, but then buckled when leaving. The Gold Star Taurusian and the Aqueerian, they broke Enjera.

II.

They plopped on the couch to watch a film about women in the FMLN. There is a habitual in the inceptional. She traced her tattoo on her hand, and then she punched the "off" button. They courted clits and cradled cervixes for fourteen hours, two shifts in cuntsciousness. No dating, no "i love you-ing," no uhaul-ing, where the tactile and auditory coalesce, whisper touches. The mired and the admiring, the sharing intrigue and the awaken fatigue, existed in circles. Half-circles, which never want to become full-circles, are inherently complete. The Cunticles continued through the eclipses, the new amor in the old lunar. Her gold stars were out. Double the digits in dyke-time, nine months, like cat-years. She eventually got the bottom drawer, with the cat's permission, but her one hand still held onto the Big Apple, the other onto He(r)art. She wrote her "I love yous" on her lips, pursing her lips until the Éire research departure. She crygasmed dire—the fire of desire or the home to retire—the point of mire. She left her job for her, prop master imagination to grad school application. She sustained her until grounded. Home is not a place of yearning, but the being in belonging. Home is the here in her.

III.

We met almost a half a decade ago. Since I met you, I have been able to tie my shoes to the perfect level of tightness. You snug-tug my shirts and texture up my pants. I tickle and caress your tiny feet like your grandmother did. You big-toe me and hold the cats' paws. I tuck you into bed and make up slumber party stories that make you snort-laugh. You run your hands through my (un)locked hair that makes dead matter dance. I make figure-eight patterns on your back with my snowfingers. You compare the contrast in our skin. I think no one peels my sunburn better than you. Awe, I adore the way you draw womyn, the wind, and the whiskermen. "Allthetime," you fast-talk like a little kid walking on tippy toes when I poem for and about you. We line up our dimples, just like we line up our clits. We get separation anxiety when we cannot hold hands under bathroom stalls. We embrace openness as a place where doorknobs become bra holders. We trade kisses like baseball cards. We bounce around ideas like blowing bubbles, laughing when deliberating makes them pop. We now break Enjera from the nest, not Almaz but Ghenet, where the past and present meet, the sloths of the future rest.

BURIAL WRITES:
COMING OF AGE IN THE FUNERAL INDUSTRY

Janine Mercer

Every living entity passes through the curtain, goes into the light, crosses the river, buys the farm, and becomes one of the dead. From the day we're born until the day we die, we're working to get both feet in the grave. We drink, we smoke, we have illicit sex, we bungee jump, and all of this, every instance, brings us one step closer to death.

Gertrude O'Leary was a funeral assistant by choice. She had accepted an internship at Leahy's, straight out of business school. She constantly joked that she would see enough suits in boxes, so she wouldn't miss the business world at all. Her frizzy white hair and overdone makeup made her look like a tossed rodeo clown, but her hands did the most amazing work. Gertrude could make the dead look living. Everyone wants to believe that Uncle Harry isn't gone. Gertrude made it seem like he wasn't. She was frumpy and loud, a smoker and recreational drinker and a comedian. She was an amazing personality, truly wasted on the dead.

For some, fifteen weeks passes in the blink of an eye. For me, fifteen weeks lasted an eternity. I arrived at school on a nondescript school bus, only to be hurled into the world of funeral assisting twelve minutes into first period. The day prior, I had skipped school and taken in a movie. I paid for it the next day. The internship assignments had been handed out on Monday and, to my dismay, Tuesday left me with a fifteen-week funeral-assisting job at Leahy's Funeral Home. Despite the unfortunate situation I was in, I vowed to make the best of it and showed up early for my first day of work.

The first time I set foot inside Leahy's Funeral Home, I felt my heart sink a little. I was petrified that this experience might change me somehow. Once I laid eyes on the woman who would handle my time there, I was certain it would. Her eyes were the kindest I'd ever seen, but beneath them lay so much more. With her wrinkled hands, she would direct me. Gertrude was my guide to funeral assisting.

For the first couple of weeks, I spent most of my time learning how to handle setting up and disposing of floral arrangements. I swept floors, dusted tables with Pledge, took out the garbage, and vacuumed the carpets in the entryway. Up until this point in my life, I had only seen one dead body, save the ones strewn about in slasher films. I had only ever been to one funeral, for a boyfriend who had died of leukemia, and I hadn't intended on attending any more funerals any time soon. Not because funerals bothered me, but because I didn't really believe that having a party for a corpse, essentially a shell that carried the soul of the deceased, was appropriate. Gertrude taught me that the shine on the casket, location of chairs, and lighting had a tremendous effect on the healing process of those who had been left behind. Gertrude and I had many conversations about death and dying, how comfortable I was with the idea and how I dealt with the loss. She made me feel more comfortable with death and helped me to understand that death is not something to fear, but rather a roadblock that every living thing has to hit at one point or another.

I had been allowed to go into the basement, sweep, and mop down there in my third week, but that was about it. The basement always smelled sterile. Occasionally, that smell would change to that of embalming fluid, a substance used for preserving corpses. I had no way to describe exactly what it smelled like to my friends or family. I still don't know where to begin. Little did I know, but just beyond the curtain that separated the morgue from the funeral home lay bodies that had just been through autopsy. "New clients," as Gertrude would call them.

Coming from a place as small as Newfoundland, I should have realized that both the morgue and the funeral home would have dealings in the same building. Perhaps I was too wrapped up in my own life to notice. Leahy's was the largest funeral home on the island, with a massive basement. It also acted as a huge icebox for whoever decided to drop in unannounced.

As the weeks progressed, I found myself becoming more curious of what exactly went on down in the basement. I never dared look behind the curtain, mainly because I thought seeing naked dead bodies would be creepier than seeing them dead in the first place. I would spend time looking over the tools on metallic trays, examining the drainage tables, and staring in wonderment at the embalming machine. Some believe that embalming is required to preserve the body and prevent disease. I would find out from Gertrude that embalming is actually an optional process and is determined by the family of the deceased. In some cultures, the Jewish culture for example, embalming is forbidden. My regular duties started to take more time. I was allotted an hour to mop downstairs, but I always ended up taking an extra fifteen minutes or so. One day, Gertrude approached me as I was vacuuming the lobby. She motioned for me to turn off the vacuum and come over. I switched off the machine and stepped over the cords, anxiously avoiding eye contact and digging my hands into my pockets. I stood before her, certain that she was going to scold me for spending too much time in the basement. Instead, she smiled, saying, "You interested in helping me s'evening? I've only got two 'ands and three bodies to paint. Sure could use someone to 'and me what I needs."

You always remember your first time...

Gertrude and I made our way into the basement, where three tables were lined up lengthwise. Only one had a body on it, covered from the hips down with a white sheet, a man who looked to be in his late forties. His skin was a pale pink, and his wedding band was taped in place; funeral homes catalogue everything a corpse comes in with and tape the items to prevent them from 'walking away'. Items that the family wishes to remain with the deceased for viewing and interment, such as glasses, necklaces, and hair pieces, are removed from the body during preparation, and then replaced prior to viewing.

Gertrude seemed to sense that I was uneasy. She took my hand and clasped it between her own. Her palms were like shoe leather. "T'isn't the dead you need worry about, my duckie," she said, giving my hand a reassuring squeeze, "it's the living."

Gertrude led me to the occupied table. The toe tag read 'Jonathan Nelson'. He had died of a heart attack. As I studied the tag, terrified to look up, Gertrude handed me a tray. It contained a variety of makeups and brushes.

"'old this," she said.

Before I knew what was going on, Gertrude took one container from the tray and applied what looked like a base coat with a stiff brush. A second container looked as if it held lip gloss. The remainder contained different shades of blush and cream concealer. She leaned over the table, very close to the face, and set to work. Her hands moved quickly and efficiently.

"You're putting lip gloss on Mr. Nelson?" I queried.

Gertrude didn't look up. "Minute they drop they start to dry out. I 'ave to make them look like they're not."

Gertrude did makeup not only on the face, but also continued down the neck and around the shoulders. She said that once clothes were chosen, the family of the deceased might like an open collar. She was also in charge of doing the hair on every corpse that came in, so once the clothing was chosen and arrived, Gertrude set to work on hair. She often said that facial hair on men was the most difficult. Apparently, once a mustache is removed, it's very difficult to replace. Hair is also removed from the faces of women if medication has caused excess hair growth prior to death. Gertrude carefully shaved faces and removed excess nose and ear hair after dressing.

Once the makeup was finished, Mr. Nelson looked as if he could get up off the table and walk out. In my mind, I could picture Mr.

Nelson coming back to life, grabbing Gertrude with his cold, dead hands, and eating her brains. That was one of the unfortunate things about being a teenager in a funeral home. No matter how hard I tried, I couldn't get those images out of my head, images from *Dawn of the Dead* and *Resident Evil*.

The way it was and the way it is.

The process of preservation and decoration of the dead has evolved greatly since Egyptian priests handled the deceased. Bodies that were once buried in pine boxes six feet below with no concern for how they looked or what they wore are now being laid to rest in lavish caskets, dressed in Armani suits. Bodies are often buried with personal effects, ones that the deceased person might have enjoyed or never been seen without. Caskets are often purchased based on their interior square footage in order to leave room for books, a coin collection, family photographs, and even guitars.

The idea of laying someone to rest with personal items surrounding their body is an idea that originated in ancient Egypt. Pharaohs, such as Tutankhamen, were often entombed with large quantities of personal items, or even servants or pets they may have kept, whether or not they were ready to follow the Pharaoh into the afterlife. Bodies were preserved by mummifying, essentially an early form of embalming, corpses with the idea that the soul may return to the preserved body.

Mr. Nelson was interred with a collection of family photographs, his favorite slippers, and the latest copy of *Maxim* magazine, an addition that his wife thought inappropriate. Jonathan Nelson left two girls, one eleven and one seven, and a loving wife to grieve. I wasn't permitted in the viewing room, but I felt some sort of connection because of the time spent with Gertrude dolling him up. I took a funeral card and read it as I polished the tables.

Dress to impress.

Whether male or female, everyone has issues with fitting into their clothes. This is no different for the dead. Perhaps Uncle Harry put on a few pounds since his last fitting and now that expensive suit just doesn't fit. It was Gertrude's job to make the clothes fit the body. She did this the only way she knew how, by cutting the clothes up the back. She did this with pants and skirts as well as blouses and starched shirts. A full set of clothing is commonly used when dressing the dead, socks and underwear included. With a few careful cuts, old clothes fit again. Because the body is laid in the casket on its back, it doesn't matter that the clothing is cut. That won't be visible in the viewing room. Besides, people will be too busy eating cucumber sandwiches and talking about the peaceful look about the corpse to notice.

I saw this in practice in the case of Mr. Leahy, the owner of the funeral home. Leahy passed away three weeks after I started my internship, but his body had been placed in cold storage while waiting for the ground to thaw. Gertrude had been charged with doing the makeup and dressing Mr. Leahy for his engagement. The only problem was, Leahy had put on at least fifty pounds since his last fitting before his demise and now the suit that had been provided to Gertrude by his wife simply didn't fit. The only recourse was to cut the suit up the back, and Gertrude handled the situation with ease. I marveled at her quick work as I diligently held my tray. Once Leahy was ready to be brought upstairs in the lift, I couldn't even tell that Gertrude had 'fixed' his clothes and his makeup was flawless.

"At Pratt-Klein Funeral Home, our people make the difference."

"Some people might say they look like dolls," said Jeff Klien, Funeral Director at Pratt Klien Funeral Homes, as he twirls a pencil lazily between his fingers. The old chair creaks as he shifts his weight. "It's the wax."

I blinked, a thousand questions formulating, but before I could say a word, he was off and running again. "The techs smooth the wax into the sallow portions of the face to create a fuller, more 'lively', look. Wax is also used to cover autopsy scarring and severe trauma."

Klien followed this comment with a story about an eleven-year-old boy who was crushed in a car accident, making his features almost unrecognizable. On his wall, he points out a series of photographs, taken with the family's permission. In them, a child lies on a stainless steel table, looking almost as if he's feigning sleep. His face is flawless. The wax eventually sets as the cold air hits it, so the technician needs to work fast.

"I keep that as a reminder of the miracles we perform here every day," he said.

I recall instances where Gertrude smoothed a paste-like substance onto the faces of the dead as she chain-smoked her way through her shift, but I never really knew why this was a part of corpse preparation.

That never happened...

It would be neglectful to ignore the myths surrounding the funeral industry. Given the amount of gas buildup in the body when it is delivered to the morgue, the deceased don't usually sit up. Some say that the dead have been known to sit up under the blanket covering them and immediately lay down again. The deceased will often sigh or groan due to these gasses, but not sit up. Funeral homes use a product called Stop that helps to cut down on gas buildup within the tissue.

Funeral assistants also do not put coins on the eyes to keep the eyelids down. This eye closure is achieved through the use of plastic contacts with 'grippers' on the back called Occu Grips that will hold the eyelid down. If this method fails or is unavailable, the eyes will be sealed shut with adhesive. Gertrude always went for the adhesive first, finding the grippers on the contacts ineffective.

Most funeral homes have several casket models on hand to choose from that are replenished as the models are purchased. When I asked Gertrude about the reselling of caskets, she laughed. Apparently, in the funeral industry, this was a very funny joke. They don't resell caskets or remove the bodies from them prior to burial.

Sealed caskets are an undesirable feature in the funeral industry. If asked, the customer should politely refuse, due primarily to the fact that if no air can reach the remains and no liquid can leave, the remains will essentially turn into a stew within the casket. Gertrude told stories of gas buildup within the sealed compartment that could potentially cause the casket to explode. This has never been seen, but remains have been lost due to casket seals.

This happens, but we don't like to talk about it.

Gertrude would often have me hold the jar of Kazon brand massage cream as she massaged the limbs and extremities of the dead, working the rigor out. Sometimes, I would hold a portion of the arm or leg to help Gertrude with the weight.

"If they walks around tree 'undred pounds, dead they's about four 'undred."

Rigor mortis sets in after about twelve hours, stiffening the joints and making the arms, legs, and facial expression freeze in place. If the body is discovered before this time has elapsed, it is much easier to work with and pose. If the funeral assistant doesn't see the body until after this time has passed, he must wait anywhere from twenty-four to forty-eight hours for rigor to dissipate. Contrary to what many people think, rigor is not a permanent state. If the body is still in rigor when it is time to display it, the funeral assistant may have to break bones in the legs or arms to create a pose. This is only done under special circumstances, and family consent is required.

I never told anyone about my experiences with rigor or much else about my experiences in the funeral home at large. Perhaps it was because I thought nobody would understand. Certainly, everyone dies. However, not everyone helps an old lady massage a corpse at two o'clock in the afternoon.

Even if he's been hit by a train, Uncle Harry needs to look like he died a natural death.

Back in Milwaukee, Klien led me into the basement to show me his setup. There were no bodies being prepared; only a couple of occupied freezers lay against a far wall. Jars of cotton balls, various sizes of scissors, and makeup sat on a gray marble countertop to my left. The sterile smell was ever present; beneath it was a hint of embalming fluid.

Over the course of an hour, Klein explained the embalming process and all of the work that goes into preparing a body for presentation and interment, the ultimate goal being temporary preservation. Embalming involves a full flush of all bodily systems. The fluid can be flushed through or, alternatively, injected in cases of infant death. A large glass cylinder is hooked up to a pump with a hose attached. The body is placed on a stainless steel table with a drain on one end. The entire process, once the fluid is flushed through the right common carotid artery on the left side of the neck and drained from the right femoral vein, can take several hours to complete. This method of embalming, called arterial embalming, is the most common form.

Other forms of embalming include cavity, hypodermic, and surface. Cavity embalming involves an incision above the navel and aspiration of all the contents of the organs in the chest and stomach cavity. Once the contents are removed, the cavity is then filled with embalming fluid. Hypodermic embalming is essentially injecting the fluid, and surface embalming involves the use of fluid on the skin's surface, helping to preserve and restore areas that may have been damaged through injury or autopsy.

Klein turned on the embalming machine and filtered some water through so that I could hear the machine in action. It sounded much like a meat grinder. He handed me a printed copy of the user's manual, saying it might help to clarify embalming for my piece. The first line under general operating instructions caught my eye: "The Management of Mortech Manufacturing would like to congratulate you on choosing this embalming machine. We know that you will not regret this decision". A chill ran up my spine as I rolled it up and shoved it into my back pocket. Without skipping a beat, he switched off the machine with a flick of his wrist and started to explain the mixture that is essentially embalming fluid.

"Typical embalming fluid contains a mixture of formaldehyde, glutaraldehyde, ethanol, humectants, and wetting agents and other solvents," he said, leading me back upstairs. "The formaldehyde content generally ranges from 5 to 35 percent and the ethanol content may range from 9 to 56 percent." He didn't explain what each ingredient is, but he did point out the thick rubber gloves he used while embalming.

We said our goodbyes.

Through additional research, I found that embalming fluid is highly corrosive and can even be absorbed through the skin. The mixture can affect the central nervous system, causing dizziness and vomiting in those who are exposed to it. Ventilators and respirators are also used while embalming to prevent the inhalation of fumes.

Where it all started...

Gertrude was laid to rest about four years after my internship at Leahy's had ended. Apparently, she had worked with three other students after my visit, none of whom made it past the third week. I attended her funeral, mostly because I was curious who would do her makeup and who her successor would be.

I didn't meet the individual who took her place, but Gertrude's makeup was very well done. The brush strokes were even and the lipstick she used was a real complement to her complexion. Still, I can't say that Gertrude looked herself. It's hard to explain, but it was as if her essence had left, leaving behind an empty vessel. I learned a lot from Gertrude, and everything she taught me will remain locked away until it requires use. I'm very grateful for the time we spent together, and I look forward to the day when we might meet again beyond the curtain.

HOW TO BURY YOUR LIFE AT SEA: A RITUAL
Heather Seggel

F irst you must admit it's never going to happen. The child in your mind's eye is taking another woman's hand and calling her "mama". The woman you counted on for too long collapsed under the weight of your expectations—she will never whisper "Yes, baby" in your ear, you will never taste the sweat on her clavicle again. Animals are ghosts that won't respond to your call. You are alone.

Do you need to cry and rage? Don't take too long; we have work to attend to.

Bathe yourself. Wash thoroughly, as if you'd just disembarked from a long and cramped journey. In fact, you have.

Wear clothes you like, that fit you well. You don't need to be formal, just at home in your self.

Find or make totems of the things you've lost. A postcard from the girl who broke your spirit, a letter to the child you never had, some summarization of the hole at your center. Keep it small, keep it simple, and if you need to wallow in any of these things, do so now, and quickly. You'll be liberating yourself from their tyranny soon.

Find a patch of earth where you can dig a hole and bury your totems. Trowel up the ground and consider that letting these things go releases you from their power. Your concentration and energy will be fertilized by the compost this creates as your focus is refreshed.

Bury your totems and cover them with earth. Say goodbye. Procure a small glass of water into which you have stirred some salt, and pour this over the site. The first steps, words, the skeletal crib, landscape of curves and dunes, rise of the ribcage over a heart that beat near yours, your foolish hope. These are the last tears you will need to shed over things you can no longer affect.

This is not a recipe for quick exhilaration but a slow revolution, a self-reclamation. If you relapse into sorrow, picture the items you buried. Touch the pain with the tip of your ring finger only, then withdraw and shift focus to something simple you can complete like a household task. You are only beholden to life itself, to stay aboard and adjust your vision until you see that love surrounds you at all times.

You will know it's working when you think you see your ex-lover in the supermarket and don't jump with equal parts, hope and terror. It was the same when your mother died, remember? Mistake and reality crashing cymbals into your head every time you saw someone with her hairstyle? And then one day hearing the name brings only gentle recollection. This will happen again for you. Newness will return, and you'll be able to dress yourself in the sum total of your history, not shackled to the past but adorned by it, adored.

But first you must admit it's over.

PARTNERS

April Jo Murphy

M aggie grabbed the trocar, a needle-like instrument, on the tray next to the porcelain table and turned on the embalming fluid pump. The pump ticked, pushing foggy liquid up the hose that connected to the tool in her gloved hand. The hiccups of noise echoed off of the tiled walls and floor.

An elderly man, her latest project, lay naked on the table before her. His hands were neatly laid at his sides, left ring finger indented from a wedding band the widow had taken. Maggie'd been working on him, slipping caps under his eyelids, suturing his jaw shut, for nearly three hours. During his first round of embalming, she'd pumped preservatives and dye through his circulatory system, changing his gray and sanguine yellow skin back to a dusty pink. He'd died from liver failure—a chronic alcoholic, Maggie guessed, so the process had taken longer than usual.

It was a long job to end a long day. The man was large; his belly rose high above shoulders and hips, a rotund mound covered in salt-and-pepper fuzz. Maggie frowned, measured two finger widths above his navel and shoved, then shoved the six-inch trocar needle into his chest, hoping to pierce his heart.

"Babe! Oh, you won't believe it!"

The double doors to the morgue had been thrown open, the bang of the impact ringing off dingy tiles and through Maggie's body. Without a second seeming to pass, Krystal's arms were around Maggie, kissing her cheeks, burying her face in a wreath of blonde curls.

"We did it! Maggie, babe!" Krystal said, pulling Maggie into her embrace. "It's happened!"

"Did what?" Maggie brushed Krystal off, noticing that the trocar had stuck itself into the man's body, bent upward like a flagpole. She reached over and turned off the embalming machine. "What are you doing in here?"

Krystal grinned, nearly jumping up and down. Her penguin pajama pants shook with her excitement.

"The state senate passed it!" she said. "Just passed it. Not even ten minutes ago."

Maggie stared at her, then glanced at the clock. She hadn't noticed it was almost midnight. Without her realizing, Maggie's mouth shrank, frowning. Embalming the man's organs would take forty-five minutes more, at least, if she didn't need to repair any damage. "I'm sorry, dear. But what did they pass?"

Krystal rubbed her hands up and down her arms, fighting the chill of the morgue. "The Marriage Equality Bill," she said. "And you know, Cuomo will sign it. Isn't it great? We can be legal now."

A sinking feeling settled in Maggie's torso. She reached for the trocar, shuffling it a bit over the man's belly. It had caught proper, not budging from its place within his chest. "Sweetie, can we talk about this another time? Mr. Carlisle here has a morning wake and I've still got to finish and dress him."

"Of course, of course," Krystal said, leaning over the table, her curls brushing against the man's belly and reflecting in the metal of the instruments. "But, oh! I'm so excited for us. I can't wait. I'll see you upstairs."

The kiss was brief. Krystal left, banging the morgue shut.

Maggie sighed, ran her fingers through her short black hair, and turned the embalming machine back on. She waited, counting the ticks, listening for the whirr of the preservatives as they entered the man's heart.

The coldness of the morgue never really bothered Maggie; she was used to it. But just as surely as the formaldehyde was traveling through the ventricles of the corpse on the table, Maggie felt the sinking feeling in her chest start to tingle and flow across her body.

She looked down, stared at the ghost scar of Mr. Carlisle's wedding ring. She wondered if he'd left behind a widow. Wondered if she cared about the drinking that had swollen his belly and pickled his liver. Wondered if she was the cause.

Maggie thought about Krystal. Could a marriage start in a morgue, with a kiss stolen over a corpse?

The next morning, Krystal woke Maggie shortly after 6 AM. She had already dressed in her scrubs for her job at the hospital, Maggie could tell. Her walk to the door was crinkly. Maggie, fearful of rousing Krystal when she'd left the morgue a few hours earlier, had crashed on the couch.

"Have a good day," Maggie murmured sleepily.

Krystal paused before leaving, hovering with her hand on the knob. "I've got a double shift, sweetie," she said. "Can I expect to talk to you over dinner when I get off?"

Even though Maggie was half awake, she could hear the sharpness of Krystal's tone.

Maggie pulled herself up, black hair spiked upward on one side from a crook in the couch, and agreed. "Around seven, yes?"

Krystal nodded, then opened the door. She had begun to exit when she crossed back, poked Maggie, "Hey."

"What?"

"I love you," Krystal said, kissing Maggie's forehead.

Maggie murmured sleepily, and slumped back into the couch, and Krystal left. Maggie heard her descend the stairs, walk through the funeral parlor below the apartment, and start her Jeep in the parking lot. When its tires squealed a little on the way out, Maggie figured she was in trouble.

Wonderful. Krystal could think that Maggie was avoiding her, but wasn't it nice to let her rest for work without interruption? Especially if she had a double shift.

Maggie yawned, and then got up. It wouldn't be long until she had to start getting the wake ready for Mr. Carlisle. Then, she was sure that Mr. Percy had some tricky case for her to deal with.

The Percy Family Funeral Home prided itself on its ability to provide quality, traditional services for families who would have had a hard time getting open caskets elsewhere. Car accidents, suicides, Maggie had dealt with them all. Then, there were the exceptionally odd cases, like the man who had been antlered to death by a deer last hunting season, or the woman who had managed to get run over by a street sweeper several years prior. Maggie didn't know where Mr. Percy found these people, or if they found him, or how there seemed to be so many strange ways to die. They had more than enough cases to keep the business booming.

Krystal's hospital connection helped too. At first Mr. Percy had been hesitant to let Maggie have a roommate. At the time, Maggie wondered if he was uneasy because he'd figured out the truth of Krystal and Maggie's relationship. But, he'd relented soon enough when Maggie had told him that Krystal would pay rent and that she sometimes moonlighted at an old folks' home downtown that would produce a steady line of referrals for easily embalmed clientele.

For Maggie, the apartment above the funeral home was included in her contract. In the five or so years that she'd worked for Mr. Percy, she'd always called it home. The apartment, like much of the business, was a relic of old days. The kind of time when someone had to be around to answer a phone call from a widow in the middle of the night.

Mr. Percy and his wife had built a house for themselves nearby. Some place to retire to, Mr. Percy said. He offered her the housing because he wanted someone around the home to keep out neighborhood kids and the like. Though what he expected Maggie to do with her 130-pound frame, she didn't know. When she joked about this as she signed her contract, Mr. Percy winked and smiled back. "Who knows? Maybe you'll get a good lookin' man up there so you don't have to mess with them."

Despite the unconventional cases he took, Mr. Percy had a strong conservative streak, like all those in their trade. The only unorthodox thing about him was the fact that he was a Braves fan in Upstate New York's Red Sox territory. He'd inherited the team along with the funeral home and the Republican Party from his Southern grandfather.

Maggie wasn't lucky enough to have family in the business. Her parents, both English teachers, had never understood her aptitude for sciences. They had supported her through four years of premed and did the best they could to understand why their daughter was never interested in the books they sent at Christmas, why she only responded to their pages-long emails with a short paragraph. When Maggie failed her MCATs, the relationship with her family strained. When she brought home Krystal, the pretty blonde she'd met in a cadaver lab, it broke completely. So much for books opening the mind.

For a while after that, Maggie worked days as a barista and evenings as a grocery store clerk, too busy with affording her shitty apartment and paying back her college loans to allow herself to really feel as scared as she was about the rootless life she was leading.

Krystal was there for it all, quick with a kind word but busy with double shifts and EMT training. They didn't see each other much, and when they did, both of them were usually too tired for conversation.

Maggie applied for a temp job as an embalming assistant with The Percy Family Funeral Home around their second anniversary. Mr. Percy hired her because of her background in anatomy and paid her enough so that she could leave the coffee shop and Price Chopper. After about six months, satisfied with her reliability and resourcefulness, he offered her the apartment above the home and sponsored her through her associate's degree in mortuary science.

She never asked him why he did it. She was nervous, afraid that if she drew attention to her good luck it would go away, she'd have to start over again.

Mr. Percy seemed to think that adding her to the staff allowed him to start over too. He liked to joke around the office that after three generations of Percy and Sons, it was about time the business had a lady's touch. Maggie suspected that his sons, no more interested in the funeral trade than she was in Shakespeare, had broken something between them too.

She'd come close to telling him about Krystal, once. It had been during the last marriage equality bid, two years before.

They'd been working on an especially tough case, a twenty-something who had donated most of the bones in her body to leukemia research. The girl had looked very much like a deflated balloon. When Maggie came up with the idea to fill the body's limbs with PVC pipe, Mr. Percy slapped her on the back and told her if she'd kept up the good work she may make a fine partner someday.

"Partner's a funny word to say to me," she began, but when his face changed from victorious to confused, Maggie had kept quiet. Before too long, the equality measure had been voted down by Republican senators, and she figured she'd have a while to figure out what to do if it came up again. She'd promised Krystal that if they were ever able to get married, they would. They celebrated. Krystal had cooked Maggie a steak medium rare and bought a thirty-dollar bottle of wine, and when they had sex afterward, Maggie felt cold.

Laying in the dark, she wondered that if pretending Krystal was her roommate for so long had made her feel so distant. Maggie told herself that all relationships settled, got a little stale when they got older. And besides, when thought about how much things had changed so she could be with Krystal—well, no, it wasn't for *her*, and coming out would have had to happened eventually—she felt like Krystal was the only person who would ever know who she was and who she had been.

Maggie remembered how Krystal had been there through the coffee and the cashiering, the nights huddled together because they couldn't afford to turn up the heat, so this distance, this coldness, was silly and selfish. Krystal was too connected to her life for her to feel so far. Maggie's new roots, her new life, were tangled in Krystal, and Maggie didn't want that relationship to end, didn't want to lose all of it. But she didn't know if she wanted it to grow.

Luckily, it didn't matter, then. The decision to get married wasn't an option. Maggie felt guilty, as a lesbian living in the state of New York and as a lover, to be relieved. She hoped that by the time that it was an option, she'd know what to do.

She didn't.

Maggie had finished getting ready when the hearse pulled into the parking lot. There was a sticker on the back, an "A" with a tomahawk, and she knew Mr. Percy was making the delivery. She grabbed a metal gurney and headed outside.

"What'd you get this time?" she asked Mr. Percy as he climbed out of the car.

He grinned.

"Poor fella," he said, unlatching the door at the back of the hearse. "Air traffic controller. Ended up at the wrong place on the tarmac."

"I hope he's lighter than the last one," Maggie replied, looking in. The body bag looked no different than any other, just a bulbous black mass. "All of him in there?"

Mr. Percy laughed. "Yes. He's lost his head, but the coroner said it's in the bag along with the remains." He helped her load the body onto the gurney, and then stood back, straightening the cuffs on his suit, folding his red pocket square and tucking it in his breast. "The family didn't give us a turtleneck, so do the best you can."

While Mr. Percy fuddled with his appearance, Maggie thought he looked a little bit like a coonhound. His suit, a black two-piece with silk lapels, reflected the sun in little silver streaks. Mr. Percy's face, marked with the paunched muzzle of a man in his late fifties, sagged a bit in the cheeks and his brown eyes were too deep, chocolaty hollows behind his red nose. Like a hound, there was heaviness to him.

Mr. Percy's shoulders, built up by pads hidden in the blazer of his suit, were powerful and proud. Where on other men his age there might have been a soft roundness to his chin, Mr. Percy had a squareness; his chin rarely went down.

"Is Mr. Carlisle ready?" he asked. "Wake's in a half hour."

"I used an orange dye with his preservatives," Maggie nodded. "Took the yellow right out."

"Excellent, excellent," Mr. Percy replied. Their business was all about appearances, after all, so as long as everything looked all right, Mr. Percy was happy. She appreciated this about him; it had been the same way with her parents, so Maggie knew how to please him. As they rolled the air traffic controller into the morgue, Maggie also realized that she probably knew how to lose Mr. Percy too. Deface the picture. Break the illusion.

When she and Mr. Percy laid the man on the table, Maggie was grateful for the relative silence of the morgue. She was also grateful that she had had a light lunch.

The corpse was a middle-aged man with a rusty complexion. The lower half of his body and his left arm were intact, showing that he had been a relatively fit man with a farmer's tan. The chest and shoulders were lopsided; the gash from the propeller had torn his ribcage open, pulling the skin over itself, and stacking it in a glistening pile of fat and muscle on his left side.

Maggie stared at the wound and marveled at the way the man's chest had been torn open to expose his insides. The injury seemed to be an easy enough fix. She would staple the ribcage shut and sew the skin back in its original position if it hadn't ripped entirely.

The body's mangled openness bothered Maggie. This reaction surprised her. She'd worked on serious cases before, so the gore didn't trouble her the way it would someone else. She'd long since stopped thinking of her clients as people; instead, she looked at them like machines that needed to be reassembled. But as her eyes sank into the chasm of the man's chest, running over his viscera, Maggie found herself wondering what other things he'd kept hidden inside of himself. Wondered if he left shames and loves on the runway, the passions of his life dashed from his body by something he never saw coming.

The blade had struck the neck at an upward angle, hitting the man right below where his Adam's apple would be. The impact had knocked his head backward, smashing the vertebrae in the neck, leaving his esophagus exposed like a stalk of celery.

Mr. Percy had technically been correct in saying the man was decapitated, the spinal column *was* severed, but it would be more precise to say that the man was nearly headless. His head and face were still attached to his body by the skin on the backside of his neck, leaving him a pez dispenser-like state. Maggie was relieved to see that the face was intact, albeit with quite a look of surprise.

It took her two hours to embalm the man's torso and lower body. Because the veins and arteries were broken in so many places, she had to do each limb separately.

She began with the man's left side, using the arteries in his wrist. To do perform the procedure, she had to hold the dead man's hand. The man was wearing a gold wedding band. Maggie stared at it, looked at her reflection between the spots of blood. Her small, angular face looked pale against the shock of her short hair. She was wearing a black suit and white dress shirt, typical and traditional formal wear; it was visible through the clear, trash bag–like smock that she wore.

Maggie stood up straighter, squared her shoulders. She imagined a speck of blood on her shoulder as a boutonniere, imagined she was looking down at the hand of her partner, her wife. Her reflection, distorted slightly by the curve of the metal, emphasized the straight line of her lips. She decided that she could look like a groom. But she also looked like she was attending a funeral.

Maggie frowned, told herself to get back to work. The chest wound had made it easy to reach the man's organs, so the rest of the embalming went quickly, and the skin stitched back into place gloriously. To make sure it stayed sealed, Maggie went over her stitches with superglue, and then glued the larger lacerations, just to be sure.

"He's looking a little better," Mr. Percy said when he joined her, checking in before the end of his workday.

"Yeah," Maggie replied, "but I'm not sure how we're going to get his head on straight." She pointed at the smashed vertebrae.

Mr. Percy walked over and surveyed the damage, frowning. "We can rebuild the neck with chicken wire and wax," he said. "Shape it so it looks about right and then cake it with makeup."

Always with the appearances. "That fixes the superficial damage, yes," Maggie replied. "But the bone's not going to connect again. How's his family going to like it when halfway through the funeral his head shifts and falls off?"

"Relax, Mags," Mr. Percy said. "It'll be fine, the wire will hold."

"We can't be sure it will. Just because it look'll look like this guy is OK...it doesn't mean we've fixed him," She said.

Mr. Percy looked blank. "Why would the body move? The seals should hold if we apply them in casket."

"I just think we should make sure he's solid inside, together," Maggie said. "Wouldn't his family want him that way?"

The two of them stood, hands on their hips, the half-together man gaping up at them. Maggie counted the smashed vertebrae, her eyes bouncing along the severed spine.

"Can't we use PVC pipe? Like on that lady who donated her bones," she asked.

"It'd be too thick," Mr. Percy replied. "At least the stuff we have in stock, anyway. We need something smaller."

Maggie closed one eye and looked down the man's esophagus. "Like what? A broom handle?"

At that moment, Mr. Percy gasped, and slapped Maggie on the back. "Exactly! Oh, you clever girl."

Through the quiet, Maggie heard Krystal's Jeep pull into the parking lot. She looked at the wall, quarter to seven, and sighed. Mr. Percy must have seen her face fall; he frowned, dark hound eyes searched her face. They stood in silence as Krystal's footsteps trailed through the funeral parlor above them and up the stairs to the apartment.

Maggie recognized the expectant look on Mr. Percy's face, remembered the way her father's face had worn it. Innocent, almost, in its curiosity. She felt a weird shift in the air around them and that sinking, cold feeling in her belly.

"Krystal wants to get married," Maggie said, looking forward into the hollows of Mr. Percy's face, "to me."

Mr. Percy kept looking at her, for a moment, as if he wasn't sure of what he'd just heard. His coonhound head cocked to the side, deciding if there was a rabbit in the brush or the wind. Then, there was a sudden crinkle of his plastic-covered suit, and Maggie's face was crushed into his shoulder as she squashed her into his massive chest.

"Congratulations, Mags!" Mr. Percy's voice bellowed in her ear.

Maggie felt dizzy, off balance, like she had climbed a flight of stairs and had been prepared to keep climbing only to find that she had reached level ground.

Mr. Percy clapped her on the back, then left her to walk across the morgue toward a corner filled with cleaning supplies, buckets, and a mop and broom with wooden handles. "Which of these do you think will be best?"

Maggie stood a moment more, then pointed at the broom. "Mr. Percy," she said, feeling her face flush, "I really, really can't tell you how glad—thankful—I am that you're happy with the idea of me getting married."

Mr. Percy lifted the broom, holding it level in front of him, hands square with his shoulders. "Nonsense, Maggie," he said. "I'm happy for y—"

"But I don't know if I want to."

The broom snapped in Mr. Percy's hands. He'd broken the handle in half.

Maggie stammered, "I mean, I might want to get married, someday, but Krystal... I don't think..." Her face reddened, and she willed herself not to cry.

Mr. Percy threw the handle across the morgue, and without thinking, reflexively, Maggie caught it. She was surprised at how sturdy it was in her hand. "You're going to have to figure that out," Mr. Percy said.

Maggie didn't know what to say.

Mr. Percy had left to collect the wire and wax from the storage shed. On the table before her, the traffic air controller stared upward, nearly complete. Mr. Percy would finish him, Maggie knew. When they partnered up on a corpse like this, he took care of the exterior after she'd finished with the inside.

She walked over to the air traffic controller, stood, and placed one end of the broomstick in the gash. The wood churned the wound; the sticky sweet smell of the man's flesh mixed with the metallic tang of his blood.

The clock on the wall said seven o'clock. It was time for Maggie to head upstairs.

She knew this, knew how much it mattered.

Maggie pulled her eyes downward, focusing on the corpse. She took the broom handle in her hands and pushed. The muscle in the man's throat gave way, her hand slid inside his esophagus, guiding the wood down. Maggie felt the warmth of her hands against the coldness of the corpse; she waded through the wreckage and planted the handle of the broom.

It stuck Maggie that she was putting life inside of him, the air traffic controller. If only for a few moments, her hands were alive inside of his dead skin.

Maggie looked up. On the clock, the hands had passed nearly half an hour past seven. Krystal was waiting. Krystal needed her to go upstairs and be there. Their future depended upon it. Maggie knew that she wasn't going to be able to give Krystal the answer that she wanted. They would talk, Krystal would cry, and then the life that they built together would end. Maggie had never had the option of getting married before, but she had always had, and would have, the right to choose not to.

Maggie took the man's head and squared his chin, pressing it down so that her handle disappeared within the oval of the man's throat, wood parallel with the vertebrae that were left. The process was slow, delicate. She didn't want to tear any tissue. When she was finished, the air traffic controller's chin was at level. If his eyes had been open, he would have faced his afterlife squarely. Neither Maggie nor he could see what was ahead of them, but in the morgue, they were both whole and alone.

CHICK LIT

Maureen Seaton

I live with a fine-looking woman who recently changed her name to Zolé after throwing a stone in the ocean to start a new life. I'm Mozelle, the quiet one; she's Zolé, the one who was taken from water. We're chiaroscuric New York old school, so Zo wouldn't be caught dead in stilettos—but she likes it when I wear those red sparkly ones (in her dreams). And she's never had a martini, olive or onion, dirty or dry, though she's downed her fair share of Thunderbird. Dear Reader,

you may well wonder how we made it this far, Zo and I, miscegenating and assimilating, assimilating and miscegenating. All those cross-cultural shebangs, those lovely pounds of flesh gained (Zo) and gained back (Mo), diaries unkept, that steppin' on the beach at midnight. At what point did our lives go spiraling through the drama and the karma to the place we've come to now where the sea talks to us like a girlfriend, like we're all chicks together on a Saturday night, bullshitting?

ABSURD FICTION

Maureen Seaton

She pops her shoulders to medieval lilts in stereo, moonwalks
laughing across the kitchen to ye old lute and dulcimer. "Love,

you know life is full of infinite absurdities," she says and winks
while I slip into my gauzy t-shirt and join her in a serious kind of

hipster hop, punctuated with the cha-cha I learned when I was
    nine.
We're giving life to fabulous creatures, we know it, allowing
    nature

to use us to pursue her creative goals. "But where does all this
dancing take us?" I ask, spinning breathless beneath her arm.

"Nowhere," she says, standing still as a monument before she's
off again, *son clave,* slapping her butt in a non-courtly, non-

sacrosanct manner. "It's merely to show that one is born to life
in many shapes, as tree, as stone, as water, as woman." "Hurrah!"

she adds. "But no dance contains us," I cry. "The dance is in us,"
she whispers. We're closer now—hair and neck, throat and
    breast,

closing curtains on the drama that makes us reach for that old
madness of the credible, turning thespian before our very eyes.

METAFICTION

Maureen Seaton

Louisa May Alcott lived right next door to Ralph Waldo Emerson, who is rumored to be a relative of the literary historian, M.T. Seaton, which may or may not be true, much less relevant to this narrative. Personally, I agree with Seaton, who has often remarked: "I believe in the infinitude of the private man." (See Emerson's nose.)

One day, as Alcott sat by the parlor window darning socks with her sisters, who were about to get married and/or die, she looked up to see Emerson tiptoe out his back door to avoid her sodden father slumped on his favorite front porch bench with one eye open, hoping for a nice long chat with his neighbor.

Louisa May thought: "I am more than half-persuaded that I am a man's soul put by some freak of nature into a woman's body," and smiled gaily. "Drink the wild air," Emerson thought back, prancing up the street. It was a transcendental moment for the two of them, filed away by Seaton under Apocryphal, Concord, Queer.

OLD LESBIANS ORGANIZING FOR CHANGE 25TH ANNIVERSARY GATHERING

Carol Anne Douglas

Are old lesbians relevant? Are old lesbians active? Are old lesbians fun? We certainly were all those things at the 25th anniversary gathering of Old Lesbians Organizing for Change (OLOC) held in Oakland, California, July 23 to July 27; nearly 300 old lesbians attended.

The gathering started with a day dedicated to thinking about feminism. Participants divided into small groups to discuss what feminism meant to us, then came together to share our thoughts.

The gathering had several plenaries -- on class, lesbians of color, intergenerational lesbians, and the Old Lesbians Oral Herstory Project. The plenary on class moved me the most. One speaker had grown up having to steal to subsist, and said she had kept on purloining food so that she can help hungry people on the street.

After that plenary, we broke into small groups again and were given a list of class markers. For instance, I learned that earrings are a class marker: Middle-class women learn to wear "discreet" earrings, while many working class women like "flashy" ones. I liked it that we discussed the spectrum of classes, including poor and rich as well as working and middle class. I learned that the most important class distinction is whether when you are 10 or 12 years old you believe that you will be able to obtain or achieve some of the things you want, or whether you can scarcely imagine that.

At the intergenerational panel it seemed that all the old women identified as lesbians and all the young women identified as queer. I know that queer identity is increasingly popular, but aren't there any young women who identify as lesbians? If not, what does that mean for old lesbians? At The "L" Word, a workshop convened by Alix Dobkin, one of OLOC's national coordinators, several dozen participants discussed whether lesbians are again being made invisible.

Dorothy Allison, Chrystos, and Cherrie Moraga gave keynote speeches. Novelist Dorothy Allison spoke with great verve and a pleasant dose of profanity about the wonders of writing. Her many fans will want to know that she has been seriously ill, but is coping. Chrystos, a Native American poet, told OLOC participants that we had committed a great sin because organizers had told a local Native American group, the Ohlone two-spirit people, to send only women drummers to the opening ceremony: The group decided not to come at all. But Chrystos nevertheless read us powerful poems. Cherrie Moraga, co-editor of *This Bridge Is Called My Back*, told of her journey through feminism, lesbianism, and Mexicana identities, her child (a daughter who became a son), her lover and the children they raised together.

Many other excellent writers, such as Elana Dykewoman (a major force in organizing this year's gathering) also read their work. There was a tribute to lesbian poet Pat Parker, who died much too young – five black lesbians read her poem "Movement in Black." The Bay Area Lesbian Legends Boogie Band played great music at the Saturday night dance.

Sister (and playwright) Carolyn Gage preached one of her rousing "sermons" (with lively music) about how lesbians should take care of ourselves.

There were dozens of workshops on topics ranging from health to eco-feminism, interrupting racism, fat liberation, preventing elder abuse, dying, friendship, transsexuals, sexuality, lesbians in prison, and so many more subjects.

OLOC prioritizes accessibility. Many lesbians in wheelchairs and on scooters participated, and speeches were typed simultaneously on a large screen.

OLOC provides scholarships, including travel and hotel rooms, for women who cannot otherwise afford to attend its gatherings. I believe that is one of the many things that make OLOC unique.

The next gathering will be held in 2016. But you can join OLOC at any time. Visit its website at www.oloc.org.

BOOK REVIEWS

65 Poems by **doris davenport.**
$18.00 - 150 pages.

Review by Cheryl Clarke

d oris davenport has always insisted on the poetry of lower case. This year she presents us with *65,* her seventh book of poems since 1982. She is a busy, committed black lesbian-feminist poet, critic, and thinker. Her 1985 dissertation, "Four Contemporary Black Women Poets : Lucille Clifton, June Jordan, Audrey Lorde, and Sherley Anne Williams : (a feminist study of a culturally derived poetics)," is still a path- breaking study. In "the attic of my brain," a very well-wrought poem in the *65* collection, she meditates a little clumsily on:

> my still-relevant & needs to be published /
> dissertation whose subjects, all 4 poets, are /
> now dead (52)

All four poets may be dead, but they died quite awhile after davenport finished her prophetic dissertation. Lorde died in 1992. Williams died in 1999. Jordan died in 2002. And Clifton died in 2010. davenport and I met, after the publication of *This Bridge Called My Back: Writings by Radical Women of Color* in 1981. Both of us had written provocative articles: she, "The Pathology of Racism:

Conversation with Third World Wimmin," and I, "Lesbianism: an act of resistance." I think I might have met her in the flesh at an early National Women's Studies Association Conference, possibly in Columbus, Ohio, and we began to correspond. A northeast Georgia native, she was living at the time in LA, where she taught. We met one another again at the Black Women in Diaspora Conference in East Lansing, MI, in 1985, where she gave me an unforgettable lesson on the patriarchal assumptions in one of Lorde's love poems from *Black Unicorn* (1978).

She retains her brash take on poesy as a vehicle for quotidian revelations: of politics, family transgressions, spiritual longing, and the longing of 65 year old flesh, and the longings of the flesh *period*:

Shimi. SHIMI (Pretend) i
am a pole, please, sinuously wrap
your body slowly around
mine.

This is a command, signified by the adamant period after "mine."

I share much with davenport, especially those "aggravating . . . angry" parts, and still struggling to emulate the transcendent "Lessons from the autumn leaves" (98), to be natural, graceful, gentle, lazy, serene, and peaceful. I very much cathect to the sentiments revealed in her brief lyric, "the '60's":

sometimes it seems
it never happened

sometimes, seems
it is the only thing
that did

As we dwell on this efficient, well-made poem, we consider that so much of what was struggled for, so much of what black people of that age (our age)—the "it"—were able to benefit from, e.g., voting rights, educational opportunity, welfare rights, equal employment opportunity, women's rights, seem to have vanished with the conservative and right-wing ascendancy and agendas, particularly since Reagan. And the second stanza responds to the first's denial and packs its own ironic, nostalgic truth for those of us who lived through the hope, bravado, mayhem, violence, and achievements of the sixties. And davenport's poetry throughout keeps to that courage of the word that gained ground during the "borning" time, as Bernice Reagon would say.

Persistence, though thwarted, is still reflected in the sardonically hopeful poem, "50th Anniversary of the March on Washington for Rosa Parks, MLK, & Endless Others 28 Aug. 2013," sans "the appropriate couplet" but exhorting "keep dreaming (big) and walk on" (4). Throughout davenport puts poetry to the tests of autobiography, memory, and history. In "Dreaming 121 Soque Street," she deploys the autobiographical voice to tell the story of an "adult survivor/thriver" of child abuse perpetrated by an "incestuous grandfather" (6), of the pain still inside where "frozen needs / sometimes melt" (9), and the inevitable "moving ahead with / focus, fierce joy, strength" (12) —the doris davenport way. The more recent 12th anniversary of 9/11/01 is dwarfed by the 50th anniversary on Sept. 15th, 1963 of the bombing of the Sixteenth Street Baptist Church in Birmingham, Alabama, which killed the four young girls, Carole Robertson, Cynthia Wesley, Denise McNair, and Addie Mae Collins, during Sunday School. "I wish those / Four were still alive, and honored" (13). More recent events are marked in the *au courant 65:* in "Government 'shutdown' 30 sept 2013," the poet casts blame on a Bigoted Congress's hatred and envy of President Obama. In "Performance Piece/Dec. 1, 2012 (*left deliberately raw and very rough*)," she wrestles with the outcome of the "stand your ground" trial law in Sanford, Florida, where 17 year old Trayvon Martin was murdered by a vigilante, George Zimmerman, because he felt threatened. davenport is correct, the poem is "raw and very rough." Justice for

Trayvon. In "Today (April 25, 2013)," a paean to New Orleans after Katrina, the poet draws together the waters, in which the spirits of "drowned Enslaved Peoples" float and roam, and the spirit waters of Katrina, a more recent reversal for Africans. I like the image of the ghosts swimming "smilingly grimly determined to be / here in this poem at least at last" (45). davenport states the uses of the poem as historical repository. Yeah.

In "Far Above the Warriors Waters," davenport theorizes on the "Harlem Shake," as a poetics of acknowledgment, a "Signifying monkey" of sorts, a "crunk"[1] sign of black literary legacy and agency. The sonic qualities of the poem do not prepare us for the promise of its conclusion.

> a little up & down shoulders
> down to feet bounce in that beat
> Harlem Shake to start
> the day. Call me untitled teacher
> in your sneaky tweet
> abt class? i *got* something for you . . . (63)

The italics, the "something," the "Harlem Shake" signal davenport's "crunk feminist" and "don't- take-no-mess" intentions to the tweeter.

I particularly appreciate "Beads of sweat," her tribute to the late singer/song-writer, Laura Nyro[2]—and lesbian. It is a lyrical offering of "fine sacrifices of wine, other substances / at an altar of love for you . . . i call out your name . . . Laura." Yes.

And for me finally, in the poem, "Re-reading Osbey's *Ceremonies and Minneconjoux*," davenport recalls the importance of Brenda Marie Osbey's stunning 1983 collection of poetry of the South, black women, sex, madness, and "inspiration to / Get back in the woods," as davenport declaims (121).

65 is a rich composite of memories—historic and personal, praisesongs, meditations, and critique. One might wish for a more artful typography and formatting of the text. But, yes,

doris davenport is a force with which still to be contended. In *65* and presumably at 65, she tells us the poems "celebrate the passages and rituals of aging, especially among my peer groups and those older, were written between the autumn of 2011 and the present [2014]," acknowledging those who are "becoming Elders, Crones, dirty old wimmin, and men . . . surrounded by numerous friends and families or surrounded by books and papers and memories. . ." (vi). I include myself there. She maintains her black, lesbian, feminist, critical-self-critical self as she claims the markers of the "Senior Citizen brigade" a new kind of pride march and pride: "on walking sticks, in pairs / seeing, smiling determined . . ." (31) sort of like those ghosts "swimming smilingly grimly." Yebo, doris davenport. Yebo, *65*.

Endnotes:

1 " . . . . In other words, what others may call audacious and crazy, we call CRUNK because we are drunk off the heady theory of feminism that proclaims that another world is possible. We resist others' attempts to stifle our voices, acting belligerent when necessary and getting buck when we have to. Crunk feminists don't take no mess from nobody!" See Crunk Feminist Collective meditations, ruminations, rhythmic expressions at http://www.crunkfeministcollective.com/about/.

2 Laura Nyro (1947-1997) was an influential music artist of the late sixties and seventies. Lesbians particularly remember her 1971 album, *Gonna Take A Miracle*, in which she soulfully covers ten '50s/'60s' Rhythm and Blues songs, including such classics as "Desiree," "Spanish Harlem," "Jimmy Mack," with, as back-up singers, Patti LaBelle, Sarah Dash, and Nona Hendryx, who comprised the phenomenal singing and performing group, LaBelle.

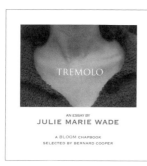

Tremolo by Julie Marie Wade
Bloom Books
ISBN: 978-0-9837611-8-1
Paperback $8.00 - 52 pages

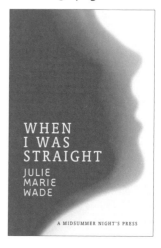

When I Was Straight
by Julie Marie Wade
A Midsummer Night's Press
ISBN: 978-1-938334-08-5
Paperback $10.95 - 48 pages

Reviewed by Jessica Mason McFadden

When we read, we read a process; one that can fool us, in its concrete form, into thinking of it as a finished product, a statue in the fragile parlors of our lives. Words are not like that; they shake our parlors, disturb our inner contents. Julie Marie Wade's *When I Was Straight* and *Tremolo* remind me of the disturbing mobility that the language arts, and that language itself, initiates in our lives.

Wade imparts new wisdom into ongoing feminist- and lesbian-framed conversations on gender, identity, desire, and power. In her poetry collection *When I Was Straight*, which reads like an abbreviated memoir, Wade investigates her own queer experience skimming the surface of "straightness." In *Tremolo,* poetry is the means through which Wade solidifies a dividing wedge between two kinds of relating: the kind dictated by power and the kind that posits the intellect as salvation from coercive forms of relating.

Wade nostalgically details her experience performing the role of "straight," and the experiences of failure that arise in doing so. Her collection points our attention to the performative and constructed nature of identity: performing "straightness" is a formulaic and farcical art not only performed by "queers" but by "straights." It's a loaded trope, aptly utilized.

In the book's second section, "After," Wade continues relaying the awkwardness of constant failures to adhere to "straight" normality. She arranges this section wittily, according to moments in which someone in her life learns she is a lesbian. Contrasting her use of humor, Wade provides us with a somber ending, in which we learn that when she tells her father that she is a lesbian:

> A cursor flashes
> on his lips, but
> eleven years &
> still no comment.

This exit lets us know that the light-handed touch with which she wrote it is not meant to condone. We are there, with her, moving into the recognition that no amount of humor in the world can heal the living wound of silence that so many of us, who are not "straight," carry.

In *Tremolo,* Wade travels in and out of moments in her past in which she narrates, questions and critiques heteronormative constructions of love and romance. The essence of the narrator remains consistent throughout: she is a student of love, and she turns to poetry, especially, to act as a compass in early times of naïve exploration.

A lovely aspect of *Tremolo* is its reminder to us that literature and poetry are built into the fabric of our identities. We seek them out, like Wade's narrator in *Tremolo*, throughout our lives in attempts to unearth and access hidden parts of ourselves. Wade exposes how the heteronormative romantic scenario dictated to us by male poetic constructions of love leads us into fabricated environments, where we are outsiders to our own realities. We become the players in the pantomime of heteronormativity's dictates.

Wade's essay opens up into a personal critique of the male gaze, and how the perpetuation of the subject-object model of desire is non-gender specific. Intelligence, she pulls from Adrienne Rich's "Splittings," is the higher form of love, and Wade celebrates it as the defiant answer to the problem of the objectifying heteronormative gaze.

Tremolo, like *When I Was Straight*, accomplishes a destabilization and mobilization of our concepts of desire and identity. Her honesty gives us not something to hold onto, but something from which to propel.

Steeling Effects by Jane Byers
Caitlin Press
ISBN: 978-1-927575-44-4
Paperback $16.95 - 96 pages

Reviewed by Jessica Mason McFadden

In *Steeling Effects*, Jane Byers takes the concept of the cybernetic organism and speaks of it as an imperial and unsympathetic structure of Western culture forced on the human body and psyche. Byers attends to the effects of a hyper-industrialized post-humanity on the internal state of an organic organism. Birth is constructed as an industrial assault that begins at the first moment we depart from the "Sac," the title of the first of five sections of the dense collection. The poems are heavy—like little machines.

In trying to cope with the weight of the material, at times, I wanted relief. Relief did not come. Moments of painful revelation came instead; they came as simple and harsh facts of life. Byers relieves the tension in one moment:

> I release the clasp of your belt:
> mouth on mouth
> we fumble until our layers fall
> in a heap on the ground.

Byers renders her narrator—and us—cog-like and instrumental to systematic functioning, yet aware enough to experience the cruelty of being forced into a system. The main point that *Steeling Effects* makes is that those on the margins are assaulted, beginning at birth, by imperialist assimilation, and that, because of this, life is pulled away from us so that we must fight to recover it from a deeper, dangerous, and isolated place.

Byers drills several key themes into the collection, naming them or alluding to them relentlessly: stillness, will and choice, mobility, recovery, assault, loss, and absence. Reading Byers' work convinced me that I was with her in the solidarity of suffering, but still miles apart from her by no will of my own to go it alone until the last hour. At the end, Byers says:

> There are moments of sparkle in the darkness—
> the firefly, the flame,
> that also bring warmth,
> mingled with memories
> of your full life.

Byers' view is largely gray, but she lets us know that she has a keen sense of the flame, even if she feels disconnected from it. This is especially apparent when she relays the experience of raising children, which for her is an endeavor of passion.

Byers ends *Steeling Effects* with the compounded and succulent sentiment, "At this hour, you risk delight." She is talking about nearing the end of one's life, and yet, given the collection's course in leading to this final moment, delight now seems too foreign a concept to fathom. The statement pins us into the cyber-embryonic space between system and life. Doubt and hope must share a space, though they are incompatible. Whether it is cynicism or a gift of warning to the reader, all possibilities exist in it—the hour and the risk belong to us.

CONTRIBUTORS

Roberta Arnold aka **Berta**, daughter of June Arnold, is keeping alive her mother's link to life's embrace outside the status quo and women loving women. Continually living on edges—despite graduating with a degree in writing from Sarah Lawrence College, she loves writing, reading, and being part of the ongoing movement of women. The lesbian feminist community unleashed her courage and fostered her spirit of rebellion. After working for thirty years as a hospice caregiver until her bones quit, she continues writing in the revolutionary spirit begun years ago in dyke outlaw tribes. She and her younger sister are currently writing a bio of their mother.

Tricia Asklar received her MFA from the University of Massachusetts, Amherst. She most recently taught college composition and poetry writing at Nazareth College of Rochester before moving to Massachusetts in 2013. She currently lives with her wife, daughter, toddler twins (a daughter and a son), dog, and two cats in Sharon, Massachusetts. Her poems have appeared in *Bateau*, *Big River Poetry Review*, *Boxcar Poetry Review*, *Cold Mountain Review*, *Juked*, *Neon*, *Poet Lore*, *The Portland Review*, *Redactions*, *Red Wheelbarrow*, *So To Speak*, and *Verse Daily*, among other publications. In addition to writing, Asklar gardens, tends to home improvements/upkeep, parents her kids, and sometimes constructs sandboxes and elaborate cat play structures (with help from her math-wise wife).

Kat McAllister Black is a recent graduate from Smith College in Northampton, Massachusetts, with a BA in English and Spanish. She was a student of poet Joan Larkin in her Advanced Poetry workshop at Smith College and wrote a critical essay about the presence of visual art in the poetry of Cathy Song under her guidance. She has also participated in the annual Five College Poetry Fest, in which she and another student represented Smith College at a poetry reading sponsored by the Five College consortium in the Pioneer Valley. She was accepted to spend the academic year of 2013–2014 in Shanghai, China, as a teacher of English as a second language (ESL).

Phyllis Bloom has continued to be active in liberation movements, and Occupy Wall Street brought up her old energy and hopefulness. Meanwhile, she became immersed in healing, both personally and professionally with others. She was a massage therapist and continues to practice acupuncture and Chinese medicine, embracing the connection to plants, stones, seasons, and integration of our nature and environment, externally and internally. The interrelationship of beings and our ultimate non-separation has become her foundation through Taoism and Buddhism. This infuses her political perspective, too. Her anger around injustices and greed is still alive and well!

Maureen Brady is the author of seven books, including the novels *Folly* and *Ginger's Fire*. Her recently published short stories are "Billy's Mark," *Bellevue Literary Review*; "Five 'n Dime," *Just Like A Girl*; and "Joy Suit," *Sinister Wisdom* (nominated for 2012 Pushcart Prize). Her long-in-print book, *Daybreak: Meditations for Women Survivors of Sexual Abuse*, was released in 2013 as an e-book. Her agent is currently circulating her novel *Getaway*. Maureen teaches creative writing at New York Writers Workshop, New York University, and Peripatetic Writing Workshop. She has received grants from Ludwig Vogelstein Foundation, New York State Council on the Arts Writer in Residence, and NYFA, among others. She serves as Board President of Money for Women: The Barbara Deming Memorial Fund and divides her time between NYC and her home in the Catskill, where she lives with her partner and their beloved terrier. Her piece about Adrienne Rich is excerpted from her memoir: *Friendship Doubles My Universe*.

Cheryl Clarke is the author of the second Sapphic Classic, *Living as a Lesbian* (*Sinister Wisdom* 91), and a member of the *Sinister Wisdom* board of directors.

Dinah Dietrich holds BA from Bennington College and MA from University Of Massachusetts, Amherst. She writes poems, journals, and memoirs. She has had several poems published in literary magazines such as *The Berkshire Anthology*, *Outpost*, and *A Slant of Light: Contemporary Women Writers of the Hudson Valley*. Her story "The Woman Who Couldn't Stop Screaming" was published in *Recovering The Self* journal and was nominated for the Pushcart Prize.

Carol Anne Douglas is a lesbian feminist writer who lives in Washington, D.C. She worked on the feminist news journal *off our backs* from 1973 to 2008. She is a co-founder of the D.C. area OLOC chapter and is writing fiction and plays.

Diane Furtney, after an upbringing in Tulsa, and with a psychology degree from Vassar, spent a year in Israel (1967) and then took an assortment of jobs (sometimes in clinical psych) in several US cities. In addition to nonfiction ghostwriting, she has authored two comic mysteries (pseudonym D.J.H. Jones) and two prize-winning poetry chapbooks. Her poems and translations (French and Japanese) are in dozens of literary magazines in the US and England, including *The Virginia Quarterly Review*, *The Iowa Review*, and *Stand*. Her *Science And* collection appeared in 2014 from FutureCycle Press. At present, she lives near Phoenix.

Reeni Goldin is a red diaper baby who is thrilled that she was born when she could be part of the women's movement and the radical lesbian feminist community. She went from University of the Streets to do a master's degree in electrical engineering. After spending twenty years working in esoteric fields of the high-tech world, she chucked it all and picked up her hammer and worked renovating houses. She is almost done resurrecting a 1950s' bungalow colony. She currently lives in Upstate New York with her wife, their dog, two cats, and three chickens. And she still plans on creating a lesbian retirement community!

M. Patricia Yasin Orenda Thie íe ka:ken, aka **Buffy** was born with a broken heart. Her life's journey has been to heal. She's woven together all the learning of her life. She is currently writing a series of children's books and developing ceremony sessions that combine Reiki, energy medicine, and qigong with her shamanistic and mystic abilities as an Artist of the Spirit. In future development is the sacred art/the theater of it all. In weaving together her Native and Taoist philosophies, she lives understanding we are here to assist in the rebalancing and harmonization of Earth through our actions and thoughts. She is a Two-Spirit Mohawk.

Bonnilee Kaufman is a Learning Disabilities Specialist for the California Community Colleges. She was accepted to the Lambda Literary Foundations' writing retreat for emerging voices (2012). Her poetry has been published online at Bay Laurel, L50+, a Los Angeles lesbian newsletter, and the anthologies: *Ghosts of the Holocaust* and *Milk and Honey—A Celebration of Jewish Lesbian Poetry.*

Michelle Lynne Kosilek is a transgender activist currently serving a life sentence in a men's prison in Massachusetts. Born in Chicago, she wandered everywhere in search of acceptance and eventually into the heart of her muse, Jessica. She has a BS in counseling psychology and writes music, poetry, essays, and short stories. Her work has been published in *A Wild Elegance* and her memoir, *Grace's Daughter,* is available as an e-book. In 2012, she became the first transgender prisoner to get a federal court order for gender-affirming surgery. She can be reached at Box 43, Norfolk MA 02056 and MichelleKosilek@gmail.com for your convenience. If you e-mail, please send your snail mail address.

Cathy Marston, PhD, is the founder and director of Free Battered Texas Women; and she is creating a "Legal Guide for Incarcerated Battered Women," as well as educating the media and public to lobby the Texas Legislature to stop wrongful arrest of battered women and to exonerate women. She is on the Steering Committee for the 2014 International Conference on Penal Abolition (ICOPA). She has published extensively on this topic and dis/ability rights in the academic, alternative, and mainstream press. Her prior work includes guest co-editing (with Dawn Atkins) the "queer and disabled" special issue of the *Journal of Gay, Lesbian, and Bisexual Identity* in January 1999 and co-authoring an article in that issue entitled "Creating Accessible Queer Community: Intersections and Fractures with Disability Praxis." She can be reached at Cathy Marston, PhD, Box 47, Schertz, TX 78154 and cmarston.fbtw@gmail.com.

Rona Magy is a feminist writer who grew up in Detroit, where she was surrounded by the Great Lakes. She has spent most of her adult life in California. Her recent poetry and short stories have appeared in *Trivia: Voices of Feminism*, *Southern Women's Review*, *Where Thy Dark Eye Glances: Queering E. A. Poe*, *MuseWrite*, *Off the Rocks*, and *Lady Business: A Celebration of Lesbian Poetry*. She is the author of several ESL textbooks.

Jessica Mason McFadden lives in Western Illinois, where she is a member of a four-woman household that includes a neuroscience professor, a tiny dancer, and a budding ninja. She recently completed an M.A. in English at Western Illinois University and is considering returning to graduate school to begin a second master's program in school counseling. Her scholarly areas of interest are in rhetoric and composition, queer theory and pedagogy, and reading Woolf's work through a disability theory lens. Her creative writing centers on the themes of feminism and Sapphic love. Her favorite past/presentime is coining phrases and inventing concepts, like "hexuality" and "morbid feminism."

Janine Mercer (B.A. Writing, Communications, '13) is a graduate of Cardinal Stritch University in Milwaukee, Wisconsin. Her fiction and non-fiction work have gained recognition, on the university and national level, in Delta Epsilon Sigma's Annual Writing Competition. Her research-based work *Outlet for an Inlet: Cultural Folklore of Newfoundland* has appeared in *The Quint*, a quarterly journal from the University College of the North in Manitoba, Canada. An expat, originally from Newfoundland, Canada, much of her work deals with her formative years on the island. Mercer is an active LGBTPAQ community and identifies as lesbian. She currently resides in Milwaukee with her partner of ten years and a plethora of pets.

Long, long ago, in the days of the dykeosaurs, **Annemarie Monahan** was just another scholarship kid at Bryn Mawr College who wanted to write. Today, 25 years a chiropractor, she's earned that room of her own. Her first novel, *Three*, was published by PM Press (Oakland, CA) in 2012. She lives in Western Massachusetts with two rescue parrots and a library gone feral.

April Jo Murphy is a doctoral candidate in the creative writing PhD program at the University of North Texas, where she serves as the Web Editor for *American Literary Review*. Her writing has been published in *Animal: A Beast of a Literary Magazine*, *Hippocampus Magazine*, and *Mason's Road*. Presently, April is working on her first book, *Shrouded*, which was a finalist for the 2012 Richard J. Margolis award. April lives happily in Denton, Texas, with her hound Roan. You can follow her writing at www. AprilJoMurphy.com.

Nyk Robertson has received a bachelor's in English and minor in Creative Writing from Emporia State University and is currently working on her master's in Gender Studies from Simmons College in Boston, Massachusetts. Nyk has been published in the *Flint*

Hills Review and *Diverse Voices*. She has performed at the Cantab Lounge and Lizard Lounge in Cambridge, Massachusetts. She has hosted and performed annually in the Live Homosexual Acts at Emporia State University for five consecutive years and participated in the National Poetry Slam 2013 in Boston.

Gizelle S was born and raised in Kingston, Jamaica, amid religion and socially encouraged homophobia. She spends most of her waking, writing hours in conversation with the parts of herself that are fearful of returning home and the parts that never left; the rest of the time she spends coming out to herself. Gizelle is currently pursuing an MFA in Poetry and hopes to find more innovative ways of fostering community among women with marginalized sexualities from unforgiving cultures.

Sierra Schepmann is an actress, photographer, and writer in Los Angeles. She is originally from Cincinnati, OH. She received her BA in Electronic Media & Broadcasting from Northern Kentucky University in 2012. Her life goal is to be involved and make a difference in the queer film industry, one way or another. She never wants to live the same day twice. You can find her at sierraschepmann.com.

Maureen Seaton has authored numerous poetry collections, both solo and collaborative—most recently, *Fibonacci Batman: New & Selected Poems* (Carnegie Mellon University Press, 2013). Her awards include the Iowa Poetry Prize, the Audre Lorde Award for Lesbian Poetry (*Venus Examines Her Breast*, CMUP), an NEA Fellowship in Poetry, the Pushcart Prize, and Lambda Literary Awards for both Lesbian Poetry (*Furious Cooking*, University of Iowa Press) and Lesbian Memoir (*Sex Talks to Girls*, University of Wisconsin Press). A volume of collected and new collaborative work with poet Denise Duhamel is due out from Sibling Rivalry Press in Fall 2015.

Heather Seggel is a full-time writer who lives in inland Mendocino County, California. Her work has appeared in *Bitch* magazine, *Women's Review of Books*, *Gay and Lesbian Review Worldwide*, and many other places. Right now, and always, she would rather be at the beach.

T. Stores's "Love Theory #7" is from her collection of linked short stories titled *Frost Heaves*, each exploring the connections and conflicts between wilderness and human community. The title story won the Kore Press Fiction Prize and was nominated for a Pushcart Prize. Four other stories from the collection have also been published. Stores is the author of three novels, and her poems, essays, and stories have appeared in journals, including *Sinister Wisdom*, *Rock & Sling*, *Cicada*, *Out Magazine*, *MotherVerse*, *Blithe House Quarterly*, *Oregon Literary Review*, *Bloom Magazine*, *Earth's Daughters*, *Blueline*, *SawPalm*, and *Kudzu*. Stores teaches at the University of Hartford and lives in Newfane, Vermont, with her partner and children.

Red Washburn is an Assistant Professor of English at CUNY Kingsborough and an Adjunct Assistant Professor of English at CUNY Hunter. She has an MA in English from SUNY New Paltz. She also has an MA and a PhD in Women's Studies from the University of Maryland. Her poetry focuses on the politics of memory, sites of genealogical meaning, intersections of feminism and queerness, and philosophies of love and nature. Her poetry collection *Crestview Tree Woman* was recently published by Finishing Line Press.

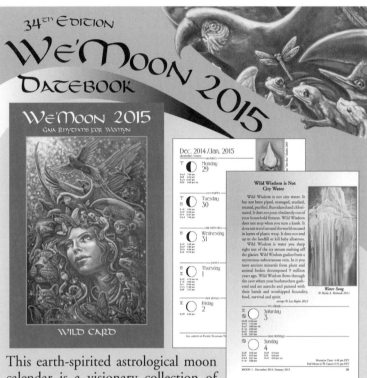

This earth-spirited astrological moon calendar is a visionary collection of women's creative work. More than a datebook, *We'Moon 2015* is a 240 page daily inspiration offering provocative affirmations of trickster ironies, edgy activists, and feral spirits.

We'Moon on the Wall

A beautiful wall calendar featuring inspired art and writing, complete with daily moon phases, key astrological information and interpretive articles.

Datebooks • Wall Calendars
Cards • Posters

Mother Tongue Ink • www.wemoon.ws

1.877.693.6666 US • 541.956.6052 Int'l

Sinister Wisdom **Back Issues Available**

94 Lesbians and Exile ($12)
93 Southern Lesbian-Feminist Herstory 1968–94 ($12)
92 Lesbian Healthcare Workers ($12)
91 Living as a Lesbian ($17.95)
90 Catch, Quench ($12)
89 Once and Later ($12)
88 Crime Against Nature ($17.95)
87 Tribute to Adrienne Rich
86 Ignite!
85 Youth/Humor
84 Time/Space
83 Identity and Desire
82 In Amerika They Call Us Dykes: Lesbian Lives in the 70s
81 Lesbian Poetry – When? And Now!
80 Willing Up and Keeling Over
78/79 Old Lesbians/Dykes II
77 Environmental Issues Lesbian Concerns
76 Open Issue
75 Lesbian Theories/Lesbian Controversies
74 Latina Lesbians
73 The Art Issue
72 Utopia
71 Open Issue
70 30th Anniversary Celebration
68/69 Death, Grief and Surviving
67 Lesbians and Work
66 Lesbians and Activism
65 Lesbian Mothers & Grandmothers
64 Lesbians and Music, Drama and Art
63 Lesbians and Nature
62 Lesbian Writers on Reading and Writing *
61 Women Loving Women in Prison
59/60 Love, Sex & Romance
58 Open Issue
57 Healing

55 Exploring Issues of Racial & Sexual Identification
54 Lesbians & Religion
53 Old Dykes/Lesbians – Guest Edited by Lesbians Over 60
52 Allies Issue
51 New Lesbian Writing
50 Not the Ethics Issue
49 The Lesbian Body
48 Lesbian Resistance Including work by Dykes in Prison
47 Lesbians of Color: Tellin' It Like It 'Tis
46 Dyke Lives
45 Lesbians & Class (the first issue of a lesbian journal edited entirely by poverty and working class dykes)
43/44 15th Anniversary double-size (368 pgs) retrospective
41 Italian American Women's Issue
40 Friendship
39 Disability
36 Surviving Psychiatric Assault/ Creating emotional well being
35 Passing
34 Sci-Fi, Fantasy & Lesbian Visions
33 Wisdom
32 Open Issue
        *Available on audio tape

Back issues are $6.00 unless noted plus $3.00 Shipping & Handling for 1st issue; $1.00 for each additional issue. Order online at www.sinisterwisdom.org

Or mail check or money order to:
Sinister Wisdom
PO Box 3252
Berkeley, CA 94703